Making Bayberry Candles

A LITTLE MAID
OF
NARRAGANSETT BAY

BY

ALICE TURNER CURTIS

AUTHOR OF
A LITTLE MAID OF PROVINCETOWN
A LITTLE MAID OF MASSACHUSETTS COLONY

ILLUSTRATED BY
WUANITA SMITH

APPLEWOOD BOOKS
BEDFORD, MASSACHUSETTS

A Little Maid of Narragansett Bay was first published by the Penn Publishing Company in 1915.

ISBN 1-55709-334-2

Thank you for purchasing an Applewood Book.
Applewood reprints America's lively classics —
books from the past that are still of interest to modern readers.
For a free copy of our current catalog, write to:
Applewood Books, Box 365, Bedford, MA 01730.

10 9 8 7 6 5 4 3 2 1

Printed and bound in Canada.

Library of Congress Cataloging-in-Publication Data
Curtis, Alice Turner.
    A little maid of Narragansett Bay / by Alice Turner Curtis;
illustrated by Wuanita Smith
        p.   cm.
    Summary: Penelope Balfour and her brother Ted find ways to
provide help to the American patriots camped near their Rhode
Island farm during the Revolutionary War.
    ISBN 1-55709-334-2
    1. Rhode Island—History—Revolution, 1775–1783—Juvenile
fiction.   [1. Rhode Island—History—Revolution, 1775–1783—
Fiction.   2. United States—History—Revolution, 1775–1783—
Fiction.]   I. Smith, Wuanita, ill.   II. Title.
PZ7.C941Lmh   1998
[Fic]–dc21   97-53230
                                           CIP
                                            AC

Introduction

IN the days of the great American revolution there was a prosperous colony on Cape Cod, and *A Little Maid of Provincetown* is the story of Anne Nelson, who lived there with some townsfolk. Her father had disappeared, and some of his friends thought he had been drowned at sea. But he had gone to Boston to enlist in the American army, and Anne, sailing there as a stowaway, was able to be the proud bearer of a very important message.

A Little Maid of Massachusetts Colony carries on the fortunes of little Anne, in which she runs away to Brewster and is escorted by Indians to her friends' home there, the Freeman's. Mr. Freeman takes her on to Boston to see her father; on the way they are arrested and locked up as spies, but escaping, Anne makes her way to Boston and helps her father capture a British schooner.

And now *A Little Maid of Narragansett Bay* is the story of the same war times, but tells of Penelope Balfour, and her brother Ted, who lived on a little farm in Rhode Island with their mother, while their father was

3

serving his country in the war. "Penny's" bravery and presence of mind were of great value to the American camp, quartered near her home, and Ted's boat, "Freedom," wins hearty praise for a share in carrying messages as well as in providing happy sailing parties.

Contents

Illustrations

A Little Maid of
Narragansett Bay

CHAPTER I

THE QUARREL

"Wait! Penny Balfour! Wait for me," called a shrill voice, and Penny stopped halfway up the slope of Bayberry pasture and looked back.

It was a day in early June, and the air was clear and pleasant, and filled with the fragrance of the wild roses which grew and blossomed all up the rough hillside. From the top of the hill, where grew the hardy bayberry bushes, one could look out across the blue waters of Narragansett Bay, with its many islands and wooded shores. As Penny Balfour stood looking down the slope she could see a little figure in a blue dress and white sunbonnet coming swiftly up the path.

"Hurry up, Florence!" she called, a little impatiently, and thinking to herself that she wished Florence Dickinson did not always want to follow her. "I don't see why," thought Penelope. "Florence has dolls, and a pony, and everything a girl could have; and she won't stay at home and enjoy herself. She's always running after Teddie and me."

Florence, seeing that Penelope was waiting, now walked slowly, and called, "Where are you going, Penny?"

"After bayberries. Mother begins making candles to-morrow. Hurry, I can't waste time. I must pick all the bayberries I can," answered Penny.

"I'll help," responded Florence eagerly.

"Come on," said Penny, as Florence stood beside her. "Mother wants all the bayberries she can get. She says it's no time to make tallow candles when there's so much need in the Colonies. And we shall sit in darkness next winter if we do not lay up a good supply of bay-berry candles."

Penelope Balfour was nearly twelve years old, and was tall for her age. Her flaxen hair was combed smoothly back from her face and the end of her braid could be seen beneath the flounce of her blue sunbon-net. She had blue eyes, and was always ready to smile, so that her brother Ted, who was two years her senior, declared that she ought to have been named Smiling Sally instead of Penelope Henrietta.

The Balfours lived in a small brown farmhouse at the foot of Bayberry Hill. There were many acres in the Balfour farm, the fields and woodland of which bor-dered on Narragansett Bay; but since Penny's father had joined Colonel William Barton's regiment to defend the Colonies against British rule, the farm no longer yielded the big crops which had made the little household secure and comfortable.

Ted Balfour was a sturdy, manly boy who did his best, but he could not, of course, carry on the farm as his father had done. He took care of the stock, kept his mother supplied with fire-wood, and in his small cat-boat often went for a day's fishing. A number of British war vessels were anchored off Goat Island, and Ted often sailed near them, eying them with hostile thoughts, and accusing them of being the cause of his father's absence from home.

Florence Dickinson lived in a big house of gray stone, about half a mile distant from the Balfour farm. There were terraces in front of the Dickinson house, and a long curving driveway led in from the highway. Here Florence lived with her mother and grandparents. Her father was in Boston, where he held an office in the employ of the English Crown.

Florence's eyes were brown and her hair, soft and curling, nearly black. She never seemed very strong, and as she trudged up the hill, her breath came in little gasps, and she held tightly to Penny's hand.

"You ought not to run like that, Florence," said Penny in a more friendly tone. "I'll wager you ran all the way from Stone House."

Florence nodded. "I wouldn't have caught up with you, Penny, if I hadn't run," and she looked up at the older girl smilingly.

"Did your mother know you were coming?" questioned Penny.

"No; she and grandmother are on the west porch, and I slipped out the east door and ran and ran!" answered Florence triumphantly.

Penny stopped suddenly.

"You've got to go straight home, Florence! Yes, you have! You know that your folks don't want you to play with me, and I don't want you, either. Your father's a Tory, and my father is an American soldier," and Penny tried to free her hand from Florence's grasp, but Florence's fingers tightened their hold, and she stood looking up at Penny with pleading eyes.

"Why don't you like me, Penny? Why don't you?" she asked.

"I do like you, Florence. But neither Ted nor I wants to play with a Tory's daughter," replied Penny.

Florence at once released Penny's hand, and for a moment the two little girls stood looking at each other. Florence's dark eyes sparkled angrily, and Penny's cheeks were flushed.

"You needn't ever play with me again, Penny Balfour. Your father's a rebel, and he'll be killed or shut up in prison, and your house will be burned down, and—

and——" Florence began to sob, and flung herself face downward on the rough ground.

Penny turned quickly and marched on toward the bayberry bushes. But in a moment she stopped and turned back. "I'll take back what I said about liking you, Florence Dickinson," she called. "I despise you, and so does Ted." There was no response from Florence; and Penelope went on and began picking the gray, fragrant clusters of waxy berries which were to be made into candles.

Usually Penny was very happy to be on Bayberry Hill, for she liked to look off toward the distant islands, to watch the ships at anchor and the fishing boats, to breathe the fragrant air, and to think about her soldier father who she knew was in camp with Colonel Barton on the other side of the bay. For days the Balfours had been hoping that Penny's father might and a chance to visit his home. But this morning Penny forgot even to look for Ted's boat. She could think only of Florence, who lay on the pasture slope angry and unhappy. She remembered how the little girl had run, until tired out, to be with her; and how tightly Florence had clasped her hand. Penny looked back, but Florence was not to be seen.

"She's gone home, and I'm glad she has. Her father's a Tory!" Penny said to herself. But the pleasure of the morning was gone. Suddenly she remembered how ill

Florence had been that spring, and hearing a neighbor say that she was a delicate child and might never live to grow up. At the remembrance Penny's own breath came quickly. Suppose she was right, after all? Suppose Florence didn't live to grow up?

Penny put down the basket and ran down the slope. "Florence! Florence!" she called. But there was no response, and she could see no trace of the little girl; and after looking about for a few moments hoping that Florence might be hiding, and would relent and come out and make friends, Penny turned and went back to her berry-picking.

By the time her basket was filled it was nearly noon, and but for the pleasant breeze from the bay it would have been uncomfortably warm. Penny pushed back her sunbonnet until it hung from its gingham strings around her neck, and started for home.

"I s'pose Florence went straight home," she said to herself, as she climbed the stone wall between the pasture and the field in which the Balfour house stood.

Mrs. Balfour stood in the kitchen doorway and waved her hand to Penny, who waved back, and quickened her steps as her mother called: "Dinner's all ready and waiting! Fried mackerel and baked potatoes, and——!" and with another wave Mrs. Balfour disappeared into the kitchen.

"I know what '*and*' means," said Penny as she reached the kitchen door, and set her basket on the broad stone step. "It means strawberry short-cake," and Penny sniffed appreciatively.

"Hang up your sunbonnet, dear, and call Ted," responded Mrs. Balfour, and in a few moments the little family were gathered about the round table which stood between the two western windows of the pleasant room.

"I saw Florence running up the path after you," said Mrs. Balfour as she filled Penny's luster mug with cool milk.

"Yes, and then she ran away from me," responded Penny, "but I made her. I told her that her father was a Tory, and that I didn't want to play with her." And Penny looked steadily at her luster mug.

"My soul, child! Whatever possessed you to turn on little Florence Dickinson like that?" said Mrs. Balfour sharply.

"And Florence said that my father was a rebel; and that our house would be burned down. And I said that I despised her, and——" Penny's cheeks grew flushed, and her blue eyes lost their friendly expression.

"There, there, child! Say no more about it. Put the butter on your potato before it cools. Ted had fine luck with his fishing, and sold Squire Dickinson a shilling's worth of mackerel. With his household 'twill be none too many," said Mrs. Balfour.

"There were ten, as good as those I brought home," declared Ted. "What a ninny you were, Pen, to turn on

Florence. She doesn't know what the words 'Tory' or 'rebel' mean."

Penelope scowled at the luster mug again, but made no answer to her brother's reproof; and Mrs. Balfour now brought the short-cake to the table, so, for the moment, they quite forgot Florence.

"Every short-cake you make is better than every other short-cake," said Ted enthusiastically, and Penny smiled happily when her mother said, "I used the round baking tin to-day; there'll be plenty for two helpings."

"I know why you did that!" said Ted. "You were hoping father would appear in time for a piece. But with those old British war vessels there's not much chance for him to slip by."

"I hope you don't go too near those ships when you are out fishing, Ted?" questioned his mother anxiously. "If they happened to think of it they would take you on board, and make what use they pleased of your boat."

"I'd like to see them catch me!" declared Ted valiantly. "Some of the sailors do know me by sight. They call me 'Sammy,' " and Ted smiled at the remembrance of the friendly jokes of the English sailors, as his swift little sailboat had sped close to the big dark hulls of the war-ships. "But I'll be careful," he added, as he noticed his mother's anxious face.

"Ted has a plan to see father, haven't you, Ted?" asked Penny.

But Ted frowned and shook his head.

"I should hope not," exclaimed Mrs. Balfour. "See his father! The idea! Don't let me hear a word of any such foolishness as that. If your father can't manage to get home it's not likely you could get to Colonel Barton's camp."

"Pen's always making things up," grumbled Ted, scowling at his sister.

Before she could reply there was a sharp rap at the door, and they all hurried toward it.

" 'Scuse me, Mistress Balfour. I'se come to fetch Missy Florence home!" and Hitty, Squire Dickinson's colored servant, stood bowing and smiling in the open doorway.

"But Florence isn't here," said Mrs. Balfour.

"She went home two hours ago," added Penny, sliding from her chair and looking at Hitty with startled eyes.

"Her mammy said she must be here," persisted Hitty. "They searched the house and the gardens, and all the places, and then her mammy says: 'Here, you, Hitty, you run fast as you kin to Mistress Balfour's and fetch Missy Florence home.' So here I is," and Hitty curtsied and smiled and stood as if she expected Florence to appear immediately.

"You must hurry back, Hitty, and tell your mistress that Florence has not been here. She was with Penelope on Bayberry Hill two hours ago, and Penelope thought she had returned home. She must be somewhere about Stone House," and Mrs. Balfour's face showed that she was anxious to be assured of Florence's safety.

"Yes'm, I'll sure tell her jest what you say," replied the smiling Hitty.

"I'll go back with Hitty—shall I, mother?—so as to be sure?" asked Ted, taking his worn straw hat from its peg near the door.

"Yes, Theodore," replied Mrs. Balfour, and she put her arm about Penny's shoulder as they stood on the broad stone step and watched Ted and Hitty until they disappeared in the shadow of the tall pines.

CHAPTER II

TED'S PLAN

"FLORENCE is probably playing about in Stone House garden, or perhaps hiding on purpose to make Hitty search for her," said Mrs. Balfour, as she noticed Penelope's sober face. "Now you pick over these bayberries, and I'll put the kettle right on, and we'll start candle-making," and Mrs. Balfour turned back to the kitchen, returning in a moment with a shining tin pan. "You can put the bayberries right in this, dear," she said, and Penny sat down on the door-step, and began picking the little stems and twigs from the bayberries.

Usually the little girl thought that candle-making was the greatest fun possible. She liked to turn the berries into the big kettle of boiling water, and, when they had boiled for hours, was anxious for what she called the "simmering" to be over. The mixture then had to stand all night, and it was on the second morning, when the wax was hardened in great cakes on the top of the kettle, that the real work of making the candles began. It was Penny who usually skimmed off these cakes, broke them up in the big porcelain-lined pan, and put it back on the stove to melt. Then, after her mother had strained the melted wax through a sieve, came the "dipping," and Penny had never discovered any game that gave her as much delight as dipping bayberry candles. The braided candle-wicking was cut in proper lengths for the candles. Then Penny would dip a wick into the hot wax. At the first dip the wick stiffened. She would hold it a moment for the wax to drip, and then dip again; and in a few moments there was a wonderful moss-colored candle, smooth and shining, a promise for light on dark winter nights.

But Penny could not fix her thoughts on this delightful prospect. All she could think of was that she had told Florence that she despised her. "And I said Ted despised her, and he doesn't. He likes her," Penny said to herself accusingly, and recalled Florence's sobs as she threw herself down on the hillside.

"Mother," she exclaimed suddenly, jumping up from the door-step, "mayn't I run up the road and meet Ted?"

"You may go and meet Theodore, but don't run. It is too warm to run," responded Mrs. Balfour, taking down Penny's sunbonnet from the wooden peg where it hung and putting it on Penny's flaxen head.

"Must I wear my sunbonnet?" pleaded the little girl. "It makes me feel all shut in. It's just as if I had blinders on. I can't see sideways."

Mrs. Balfour smiled, but shook her head. "Of course you must wear it. What are sunbonnets for?" she replied. And Penny started off toward Stone House, thinking to herself that sunbonnets were chiefly for the purpose of making little girls uncomfortable.

"P'raps Florence has run away," Penny thought to herself, with a little thrill of terror. "P'raps she has run off to her father in Boston, and dreadful things will happen to her."

Penny was now in the shadow of the woods, and suddenly a voice called, "Rebel! Rebel! Rebel!" and she stood still in amazement.

"Florence!" she exclaimed. "Oh, Florence, I'm sorry I was so hateful to you. Don't hide! Come out to the path."

"Rebel!" the shrill voice called again. But Penny was again her smiling self. Florence was safe, and Penny did not mind being called a rebel; she was rather proud of it. So she sat down at the foot of a big pine and leaned against it, feeling sure that Florence would soon appear.

"Hurry, Florence," she called. "I have lots to tell you. Something lovely."

At this a glimmer of a white sunbonnet showed above a bunch of shining laurel bushes, and Florence made her way to the path.

"What is it that's lovely?" she demanded, standing on the opposite side of the path and looking at Penny with startled eyes.

"Come over here and sit down, and I'll tell you," responded Penny, and Florence came a step or two nearer, then paused uncertainly. But Penny had already begun: "It's candle-making," she said, "to-morrow. And you can come and help dip, if you want to. And in the afternoon Ted will take us for a sail!"

"Honest?" demanded Florence, who had seated herself very close to Penny.

Penny nodded. "Yes, honest. And Ted likes you, Florence, and I like you." But Penny did not look at her little friend, for she was thinking to herself that Florence ought not to forgive her so easily.

Then, all at once, the head in the white sunbonnet was in Penny's lap, and Florence was sobbing: "Oh, Penny, I was going to hide in the woods and starve, just to make you sorry; and you liked me all the time."

"Of course I did. I was just cross," responded Penny.

"I am 'most starved now," said Florence, lifting her head and wiping her eyes.

"You must hurry right home. I'll go with you," said Penny, and the two girls started along the pleasant woodland path holding each other's hand and making plans for the next day.

When they left the shade of the pines and came in sight of Stone House they could see people moving about on the terrace and in the gardens; and Penny saw Ted wave his hat. Then Squire Dickinson, followed closely by Florence's mother, came hurrying toward them.

"It's my fault," Penny called out before the squire reached them.

"I don't doubt that," answered the squire gruffly; "like father like child."

"It isn't her fault!" declared Florence. "I hid in the woods and Penny found me and brought me home."

"What made you hide?" questioned Mrs. Dickinson, putting her arm about the tired little girl and leading her toward the house.

"Yes, tell us that," said her grandfather; and the three moved away, quite forgetting Penny, who stood looking after them.

"Come on home, Pen; they don't want us," said Ted, and the brother and sister turned and started toward home. But in a moment they heard Florence calling and turned.

"Pen-ny, I'll come to-morrow," she called, and Penny called back: "All right," and then she and Ted went on.

"She's queer, isn't she, Pen, to keep running after you all the time? What is she coming to-morrow for?"

"To help make bayberry candles," answered Penny; and then, after a moment's silence, she added, "Won't you take us out sailing in the afternoon?"

Ted chuckled. "I'll bet you promised Florence to take her sailing," he answered.

"Yes, Ted, I did. I was so hateful to her this morning that I wanted to do something, and I knew she would like that the best of anything. You will take us, won't you, Ted?"

"Her folks won't let her come; you'll see, Pen," he replied. "The squire is a regular Tory, and he hates father because he has joined the American army. He doesn't want Florence to play with you, anyway."

"But he buys fish of you, Ted, and he wouldn't let the British sailors trouble our stock. You know mother says it is a great protection for us to have Squire Dickinson for a neighbor," answered Pen.

"Well, perhaps it is. I'll take you sailing if you want to go. I wish you were a boy, Pen; then we'd manage to see father."

"Why can't I help now?" questioned the girl. "I'm almost as big and almost as strong as you are. What's the reason I can't do anything that you can do?" and Penny stopped short and waited for Ted's answer.

"Well, 'Smiling Sally,'" laughed the boy, "I guess it's your clothes and long hair. How could a sailor wear a sunbonnet?"

"I hate sunbonnets," responded Penny, and they walked on. Ted's thoughts were of a possible chance to sail across the bay to Tiverton for a visit to the American camp; and Penny was wondering to herself if there was any way to escape sunbonnets, and resolving that she would prove to Ted that she was as brave and as capable as he was. Just how she could accomplish this she did not know, but the opportunity was nearer than she imagined.

"There's mother!" exclaimed Ted, taking off his hat and waving it, and calling: "Florence is safe at home," and in a moment they had reached Mrs. Balfour and were telling her of Squire Dickinson's words when Penny had said that it was her fault that Florence had caused them so much anxiety.

"You could not do better than to be like your father, Penelope," responded Mrs. Balfour. "Squire Dickinson was paying you a compliment."

"I wish I could be just like him," declared Penny.

"Then do not trouble about what Squire Dickinson said. He has always shown himself a kind neighbor, and he does not find it easy to be a Tory when so many of his neighbors are loyal Americans," said Mrs. Balfour.

"Florence is coming to help make candles to-morrow," said Penny, "and Ted is going to take us for a sail in the afternoon, if you're willing, mother," and Penny smiled, quite sure that her mother would give her consent. But Mrs. Balfour shook her head.

"I do not believe it is safe for you children to be out in the boat, especially as Ted goes so near the British vessels," she replied.

"But, mother, they wouldn't trouble us. And if they did, Squire Dickinson would soon let them know that Florence was English," said Ted.

"She would let them know that herself," laughed Penny.

"I will see when to-morrow comes," said Mrs. Balfour, and Ted and Penny smiled at each other, for they were both sure that their mother would not prevent their going.

At supper-time Penelope was so absorbed in her own thoughts that she really did not know what her mother and Ted were talking about, and as she helped her mother clear the table and wash the blue-bordered dishes she had hardly a word to say.

"You are all tired out, dear child," Mrs. Balfour said, as Penny gave a long sigh. "You had best go early to bed," and the little girl was quite ready to obey.

Ted was busy with the milking, and Mrs. Balfour was setting out the big yellow bowls into which she would strain the milk, when Penny mounted the narrow stairs to her own room. The long June twilight filled the chamber with a pleasant light. From her window she could see the pine woods, and get a glimpse of the chimneys and roof of Stone House. For a moment Penny stood looking out, then she tiptoed carefully to the door and crossed the narrow passage to Ted's room.

"If mother hasn't cut them up for carpet-rags, she whispered to herself, as she rummaged through a red sea-chest which stood at the foot of Ted's bed. In a moment she had pulled out a pair of boy's well-worn gray homespun trousers; and now Penny smiled happily as she cautiously closed the chest and hurried back to her own room. She put the trousers under the straw bed, and then slipped off her stout shoes and cotton dress, and made ready for bed. She had planned to lie awake until Ted and her mother were safe in bed, and then dress herself in her brother's outgrown clothes. Then, if she looked as much like a boy as she hoped to do, she was sure that she would have the courage to carry out her great plan of taking her brother's boat, crossing Narragansett Bay, and visiting her father. If Ted would consent to let her go with him, all the better; but if he would not Penny had resolved to go alone. But the day had been a very busy one, Penny was tired, and she had been in bed but a few minutes when she was fast asleep, and when she awoke the morning sun was shining into the room, and she could hear her mother moving about in the kitchen; and in a moment Ted was calling: "Time to get up, 'Smiling Sally.'"

CHAPTER III

A RESCUE

"WHAT time is Florence coming?" asked Mrs. Balfour, as she helped Penny to the oatmeal porridge and milk which was their usual breakfast.

"I don't know," answered Penny. "She just called to me that she would come."

"I'll bet the squire won't let her," grumbled Ted.

But Penny had hardly finished helping her mother with the morning's work of putting the little house in order when she saw Hitty and Florence coming across the field.

"Goody! Goody! Here's Florence!" she called, and ran to the door to welcome her.

"Missy Florence can stay till three o'clock this afternoon," explained the smiling darkey, "then I'll come an' fetch her home."

"I don't want you to come, Hitty!" declared Florence. "I can go home by myself."

Hitty nodded, but repeated that she would come at " 'xactly three o'clock," and before Florence could make any further objections Hitty had started briskly toward home.

"How nice you look, Florence!" exclaimed Penny admiringly, looking at the crisp white linen dress, with its embroidered flounce and lace-bordered neck that Florence wore. "But I'm afraid you won't have as good a time in that dress," she added, a little regretfully.

"Why won't I?" questioned Florence.

"Because you'll have to be careful. You'll have to be thinking about your dress all the time," answered Penny, who had never possessed such a dainty dress, even for Sunday wear, as Florence now wore.

"Oh, I shan't be careful of this," declared Florence. "Grandma made it, and she is always making me white dresses. Mother says I outgrow them before they are half worn out. If I were as big as you, Penny, I'd give you some of my dresses."

A little angry flush came into Penny's cheeks, but she did not forget that Florence was her guest, and she had made a firm resolve that she would never quarrel again with a girl younger than herself. So she answered pleasantly: "Thank you, Florence, but I have lots of dresses. Lots and lots!" and pretended not to see Florence's surprised look. For Florence knew as well as Penny did that Penny had but two well worn cotton dresses, and the stout flannel winter dresses of brown, plaided by a scarlet thread. But the hot bayberry wax was waiting, and both little girls were soon busy and happily occupied in dipping the cotton wicks. Now and then a splash of hot wax fell on the aprons which Mrs. Balfour had tied around their necks. By the time the candles were finished and carried into the cool cellar the little girls were very warm and tired, and quite ready for a spice cake and a glass of cool milk, which they enjoyed sitting on the broad door-step. The midday meal would not be ready for an hour, so when the milk was finished Penny suggested going down to the shore to look at Ted's boat.

"Are we going sailing after dinner?" asked Florence as they stood on the smooth beach of the sheltered little cove where Ted's boat was pulled up just above the high-water mark. "What a funny name for a boat!" exclaimed Florence, reading the letters painted on the side of the boat. "'M-O-D-E-E-R-F.' Is it an Indian name?"

"Your grandfather said it was when he read it," answered Penny, looking down. "Ted says we'll sail out toward Prudence Island after dinner."

"I've never been sailing!" declared Florence, her eyes sparkling at the thought of the delightful experience that was before her.

"Florence Dickinson! What a shame!" exclaimed Penny, who could row a boat as well as Ted, and who was quite sure that she could manage the sail if Ted would only let her try. "We'll have a little row before dinner," Penny declared. "Come help me push the boat into the water."

The tide was already lapping the stern of the "Mod-eerf," and it was an easy matter to float the small boat.

"You hold her while I get the oars," said Penny, running up the shore to the bunch of low-growing spruce trees behind which Ted usually hid them. "Now climb in, Florence," she commanded, after the oars were in the boat.

Florence obeyed, and Penny quickly followed her. Picking up one of the oars she pushed the boat clear from the shore, and then skilfully made ready to row.

"Oh, Penny, you can do anything, can't you!" exclaimed the happy Florence, looking at her companion with admiring eyes.

"I can do more without a sunbonnet than I can with one," replied Penny, who had left the blue sunbonnet on its peg, and was at that very moment vowing to herself never to wear it again. "We won't go out of the cove," Penny continued. "I'll just row you to the point and back, because there won't be time to go far before dinner."

The point was a low projection of rocks which formed one side of the cove. As Penny rowed toward it the smile faded from Florence's face, and she leaned forward, her eyes fixed on something which Penny, facing her, could not see.

"What is it, Florence? What is it?" she asked sharply, at the same moment resting on her oars and looking over her shoulder. "Ted!" she gasped, picking up the oars and rowing with all her strength.

"He's gone!" gasped Florence.

In an instant Penny had shipped her oars. "You sit right still, Florence," she commanded, and rising carefully to her feet she slid over the side of the boat and struck out toward a widening circle in the water where Ted had disappeared. At the first stroke she saw him come to the surface and her voice rang across the quiet water, "Kick, Ted, kick," for she remembered the many lessons their father had given them in the art of taking care of themselves in swimming. In a moment she was near enough for Ted to rest his hand on her shoulder.

"Cramps," he whispered.

"It isn't very deep, Ted. Keep your head up. I'll tow you in."

Penny was holding Ted's head well above the water. Both the children had been taught not to lose their presence of mind in case of emergencies, and now it served them in good stead. Treading water and keeping Ted's head clear Penny made slow progress toward the boat where Florence sat frightened and helpless. "Grab hold of Ted's shoulder when he gets near enough," Penny called out.

Ted was breathing with great difficulty, but he managed to grasp the side of the boat and with the help of Florence and his sister clambered over the side and fell in a shivering heap. "Row to the point," he whispered.

Fortunately the point was but a few yards distant, and as the boat touched the shore Ted scrambled out and ran to the place where he had left his clothes. He often took a swim after his morning work and this was his first mishap. As he rubbed himself vigorously with his cotton shirt and then slipped on his homespun trousers he said to himself that Penny was the bravest sister in the world.

"I'd have gone under for good, Pen, if you had waited another minute," he said as they again took their places in the boat.

Penny, her skirts and hair still dripping, insisted on being oarsman. "It was Florence who saw you first," Penny responded. "Oh, Florence, your pretty dress is all wet," she added, looking at the drabbled linen flounce which had been so smooth and white an hour ago.

"I don't care. What's a dress?" said Florence. "Just think, Penny, if you had not been able to swim Ted would have drowned."

"Pen's all right!" declared Ted. "She can do anything; she's just like father."

Penelope was too happy to notice the discomfort of her wet clothing. To have Ted safe, and giving her the highest praise that it was possible to give any one made her smile more than ever. "Now," she thought to herself, "Ted will let me go with him when he goes to see father."

"For pity's sake, Penelope! What have you been doing?" exclaimed Mrs. Balfour as the dripping little figure stood in the kitchen door. "Here you are, wet as a drowned kitten, and looking perfectly delighted with yourself."

"Pen pulled me out of the water," explained Ted.

"She saved his life!" declared Florence; and Mrs. Balfour's questions soon brought out all the story.

She hurried Penny up-stairs to put on dry clothes, and then turned to Ted.

"Theodore, I do not want you to go in swimming alone, or unless some older person is near at hand," she said in a serious tone.

"Oh, mother!" objected Ted. "I can't always hunt up somebody when I want to swim."

But Mrs. Balfour was in earnest, and at last Ted promised.

Neither Florence nor Penny wanted to go sailing that afternoon, and Ted was not feeling his usual energy. He threw himself down on the comfortable lounge in the sitting-room as soon as he finished dinner, and when Hitty came to take Florence home he was still sleeping soundly.

"He will wake up feeling as good as new," Mrs. Balfour said when Penny tiptoed into the sitting-room and came out saying that he was fast asleep. "We'll take our knitting and sit under the big oak," said Mrs. Balfour.

Both Penny and her mother were knitting woolen socks for the American soldiers, and many other women all over the land were doing the same; but all were not knitting for the Americans, or "rebels," as the English called them, for many of the settlers sympathized with the Tories, and were eager to defeat the Americans, and to give their help to the English, under whose rule the Colonies had enjoyed so much prosperity.

The big oak was but a short distance from the Balfour house. It was a huge tree, measuring many feet in girth, and its wide-spreading branches made a pleasant circle of shade. Mr. Balfour had fixed a wide seat about the trunk of the tree, and Penny and her mother liked to sit there with their work on warm days. A few years ago it had been Penny's playhouse, where she brought her rag dolls and her bits of broken china. But Penelope was nearly twelve now, and was quite sure that she had outgrown dolls and playhouses, although now and then she would ask Florence to bring her beautiful dolls to "Oak House," as they called the tree, and Penny would bring out her loved rag doll, which she had named "Martha Washington," and quite forget that she was so nearly grown up.

From their seat under the oak tree Mrs. Balfour and Penny could see a bit of the highway that led to Warwick. Penny was telling over the adventure of the morning, and their busy needles made a pleasant sound as they darted quickly back and forth. Suddenly Mrs. Balfour stopped knitting and pointed toward the road.

"Look, Penny!" she said. "There is a party of mounted soldiers coming this way."

"Perhaps father is coming," exclaimed Penny, coming nearer to her mother and looking eagerly toward the road.

"No," responded Mrs. Balfour sadly. "American soldiers cannot ride in scarlet coats and plumed hats, as these men ride. They are British soldiers."

"Will they come here, mother?" asked Penny anxiously.

"Unless they are bound on a visit to Stone House," replied her mother.

But these soldiers were not bent on a visit; as they came nearer Mrs. Balfour could see that before them they were driving a small flock of sheep and several cows.

"Put your knitting under the seat, Penny, and run and do exactly as I tell you. Hurry! Run into the field and drive both the cows into Squire Dickinson's pine woods. Drive them in as far as you can and stay there with them until Ted or I come for you. Run!"

Penny thrust her big ball of gray wool and the half-finished sock under the seat and darted away. Mrs. Balfour hid her own work, for she knew of more than one loyal American woman whose knitting had been snatched from her hands by a British soldier. She left the shade of the tree and walked toward the stone wall which separated the Balfour place from the road, and when the driven sheep and cattle were abreast of the wall she stood at the gate watching them go by. Two soldiers were driving the creatures along at a good pace, while behind them a young officer with three other soldiers rode more slowly. It was evident they meant to stop at the Balfour farm. The cattle and the two soldiers passed, but the young lieutenant and his men drew rein directly in front of Mrs. Balfour. The officer touched his cap with a graceful salute.

"This is a fine country for good cattle, madam," he said smilingly. "If you are a loyal woman you will be glad to help the English army by the gift of a few sheep or a fat steer or cow; and if you, by unfortunate chance, are the wife or daughter of a rebel, we shall rejoice to take whatever we can." His companions laughed, and the young officer smiled as if pleased at his own wit.

Mrs. Balfour received his salutation with grave courtesy. "You will find neither fat steer nor cow in my barn or pasture," she replied. "I have indeed a half-dozen sheep feeding on Bayberry Hill, and I would ask you to spare me those, that I may spin their wool and weave garments for my little son and daughter. Squire Dickinson can better provide you."

"Indeed he can," replied the officer. "He is a good Tory, and will no doubt give us a few sheep when we ask him. But we'll not stop today; and you may keep your sheep, madam, till we are in greater need," and with a bow the young soldier and his men rode on.

Mrs. Balfour watched them out of sight, thankful that they had spared her the search that soldiers had made of some of her neighbors' places.

"Wake up, Ted," she said, hurrying into the house, and the boy's eyes opened. When his mother told him of the soldiers' visit, and of Pen's driving the cows off to their neighbor's woods he almost believed it to be a dream; but his mother told him to go after Penny, and drive the cows to the barn.

"We cannot always hope to be so fortunate," she said. "Some day they will drive off all our stock, and then we shall have to make shift as best we may."

"Perhaps the Americans will drive the British away soon," responded Ted hopefully.

Pen recognized her brother's whistle and answered it, and the bewildered cows were headed toward their stable.

"Hasn't it been an exciting day, Ted!" exclaimed Penny. "I wish I could have heard mother talk to the British soldiers."

"I'd like to talk to them," declared Ted, putting his shoulders back, and trying to look as much like a soldier as possible. "I wish Colonel Barton would send General Prescott about his business and leave the Colony in peace."

"Do you s'pose father will ever come home?" questioned Penelope in so sober a voice that Ted looked toward her wonderingly.

"Of course he will, 'Smiling Sally.' We'll go and see him soon, and find out all he can tell us. When we bring mother all sorts of messages she'll be glad we went," and Ted nodded confidently.

Pen's face brightened at her brother's words. "You won't go without me, Ted, will you?" she pleaded.

"We'll see," answered the boy; but Penny felt quite sure that Ted meant for her to go with him, and was eager to know when he meant to start, and all about his plans. They were now in sight of the barn, and saw their mother coming to meet them, so no more was said of the great adventure they had in mind.

CHAPTER IV

AN IMPORTANT PAPER

EARLY the next morning Squire Dickinson appeared at the Balfour farm. He had seen the English soldiers pass on the highway, and very much feared that his neighbor's cows and sheep had been driven off. " 'Tis a pity a man so worthy in other ways as Peter Balfour should be a rebel to his King," thought the old Tory as he approached the pleasant farmhouse. For, as Mrs. Balfour had told her children, the squire was a good neighbor.

Ted was busy hoeing the weeds from his flourishing vegetable garden, and the squire stopped to question him as to the soldiers' visit. In one hand the squire carried a small package, and, as he saw Ted, he slipped it into the big pocket of his full-skirted coat.

"Mother says that the young officer was polite," Ted admitted, rather unwillingly, in answer to the squire's questions, "and they did no harm."

"You can trust an English officer!" declared Squire Dickinson, straightening his thin shoulders. He was a tall, slender man, with closely cut gray side whiskers and keen gray eyes, and as Ted looked at him the boy thought to himself that the squire probably looked

40

like the English Dukes who wished to keep America as a colony.

"After they get all they want," Ted responded. "They were driving a lot of cows and sheep, so spared ours. But they'll come again."

The squire scowled at the "young rebel," as he called him in his thoughts, but answered that he was glad Mrs. Balfour's cows were safe.

"Will you be sailing about the harbor this afternoon, Theodore," he questioned, "in the 'Modeerf'?"

Ted always smiled when the squire mentioned the boat's name, for he could imagine how the old gentleman would scowl if he knew that "Modeerf" was the word "Freedom" reversed. Penny was the only one in the secret, and when people said they supposed "Modeerf" must be one of the old Indian names, the brother and sister were very quiet, and made no response.

"If you are going out I'd like to sail with you," continued the squire. "My own boat is too big and clumsy for me to manage, and black Aleck is busy."

Ted was so fond of sailing that he did not think it at all strange that Squire Dickinson should want to go with him, and was rather pleased at the suggestion, and answered cordially:

"Yes, indeed, sir, if you don't mind Penny's going. I promised to take her."

"Not at all!" said the squire. "I'll be at the cove at whatever time you say."

"About two o'clock, sir," said Ted, and the squire, saying that time would suit him, walked slowly back to Stone House.

Ted worked on at his hoeing until Penny came to bring him a cool drink. "Mother says not to hoe much longer," said the little girl; "the sun's too warm."

"I like it," declared the boy, "but I'll come up to the house when this row is finished. What do you think, Pen? Squire Dickinson wants to go sailing with us this afternoon."

"What for?" questioned the little girl.

"Oh, just for a sail, I suppose," said Ted.

Penny wondered to herself why the squire should want to sail in Ted's little boat, but neither of the children imagined the real reason. Had Ted known that the little packet in the squire's coat pocket contained a letter to General Prescott warning him that the American soldiers were planning to recapture Newport, and that the squire meant to have Ted sail him near enough to one of the British vessels to get the letter on board, Ted would not have welcomed the squire's company.

When Mrs. Balfour heard of the squire's request she seemed pleased. "Perhaps he wishes to let those British sailors see that you have friends, Ted. It is a kind thought, for your boat will not be over-comfortable for the squire," she said.

Just before two o'clock Ted and Penny were at the cove. Ted put up the mast, put the oars under the seats, and hoisted the sail. The little boat was ready to put

off as soon as the squire appeared, and he was prompt-
ly at hand.

Penny, who had again left her sunbonnet on its peg
behind the kitchen door, sat in the bow, Ted was in the
stern, and the squire on the middle seat. It was not a
very comfortable seat. There was hardly room for his
long legs, and he had to move often to avoid being hit
by the boom, as Ted brought the boat about to catch
the wind. Nevertheless the squire seemed well pleased,
and spoke of the fine harbor, complimented Ted on his
skilful management of the boat, and told Penny she
ought to have worn her sunbonnet.

As he moved about on his seat the edge of a thin
package showed above the top of his coat pocket. It
worked up until Penny, who faced the squire's back,
could see that it was a letter. As the little girl watched
it, wondering if she ought to tell the squire that a
package was nearly falling from the pocket of his
coat, her eyes became fixed upon the words written
across it in the squire's bold hand. "Concerning Barton's Rebel Troops," read Penny. "Forward to General Prescott."

"Oh!" exclaimed Penny, in such a tone of horror
that the squire twisted about sharply to look at her, and
Ted asked:

"What's the matter, Pen?"

"Nothing," stammered Penny, who had seen the
packet drop from the squire's pocket at his sudden
turn. It lay close to her feet.

Ted was watching the sail, the squire's back was toward her, she stooped and picked it up, holding it close in a fold of her cotton dress, and wondering what she should do with it.

The "Modeerf" was now going swiftly before the wind straight toward one of the British vessels. The squire smiled to himself, thinking the "young rebel" was playing into his hands in good shape.

"Going to run down the king's ship, Theodore?" he asked.

"I'd like to, sir," responded Ted.

"Let's see how near you can run," continued the squire still smiling, and reaching into his pocket for the letter.

As Penny saw this movement she gave a little shiver of fright, for she thought he would at once discover his loss and begin a search. Penny now understood the squire's plan as well as if he had told it to her. The package that she held so closely in the folds of her cotton dress was information about her father's regiment which Squire Dickinson meant to give to one of the British sailors. And he had asked to come in the "Modeerf" for that purpose. Penny forgot all the squire's past kindness; she forgot that he was Florence's grandfather. She looked at his thin shoulders and whispered, "Tory, Tory," under her breath, thinking of her old neighbor only as a man who wanted to harm her father, and betray her country.

The "Modeerf" was now very close to the British ship, that swung idly at anchor in the pleasant harbor. Several sailors were leaning over the side watching her approach.

"Hello, Sammy! Coming to call?" called one of the men.

"They mean me, sir," explained Ted. "I often come near as this."

The squire raised his hat. "God save the King!" he called.

"Aye, aye, sir. God save the King!" responded the men.

Ted's face flushed angrily. He did not think it was fair of the squire.

"Bring your boat alongside, and we'll make them a visit, Ted," suggested the squire, whose hand had gone back to his pocket again, and to Pen's amazement drew out another blue packet so exactly like the first that she tightened her clasp to be sure that in some strange manner it had not traveled back to the squire's pocket.

"No! No! Don't, Ted!" Pen exclaimed.

The squire turned his head to frown at her, and then brought out from his pocket a number of good sized pebbles; tying these with the packet into his big silk handkerchief he stood up in the boat and hurled it through the air. It went over the ship's rail and struck the deck.

"A note for your captain, my good men," called the squire.

At that moment Ted brought the boat about so sharply that the squire stumbled, clutched at the mast, and nearly upset the boat. He muttered angrily at Ted's clumsiness as he regained his seat. But Ted made no answer. He thought to himself that now he understood the squire; he had used Ted and the "Modeerf" to carry information to the British.

If Ted had known that the paper hurled aboard the British vessel was a list of groceries needed by the squire's household, and addressed to a Providence grocer, he would have been as pleased as the ship's captain was puzzled.

Ted sailed straight for home, and no word was spoken until the squire stepped on shore.

"Much obliged," he said; "glad to get a chance to send a word of greeting to my English friends," for he did not for a moment imagine that either Ted or Penny had suspected his errand.

Ted busied himself with the boat until the squire was out of hearing; then he turned to Penny, and the little girl realized that Ted was more angry than she had ever seen him.

"Do you know what the squire has made me do?" he exclaimed angrily. "He's made me take him out near enough to that old vessel so he could throw some message aboard."

"That's what he thinks he has made you do," responded Penny, "and he did throw something, but this is what he thought he was throwing," and she held out the blue covered packet toward her brother. Ted grasped it eagerly, and began reading the inscription aloud.

"Hush!" warned Penny, and he finished reading in silence. Then Penny told him how it had worked out of the squire's pocket, and how she had hidden it in the folds of her dress.

"Colonel Barton ought to have this right away," decided Ted. "When that captain finds out that the paper doesn't amount to anything he'll come ashore and ask the squire about it. Penny, I'm going to sail over to Tiverton to-day and carry this paper to Colonel Barton."

"I'm going too," said Penny. "You promised. Are you going to tell mother, Ted?"

"No, Pen, mother mustn't know, for the squire is sure to question her, and it would be a lot better if you would stay at home," said Ted.

"They would question me. Like as not the squire would ask me if I had seen a blue packet," responded Penny.

"That's so," agreed Ted, "but we mustn't waste time. We must start right off. What will we do with this paper?"

Pen suggested Ted's blouse as a hiding place, or her own dress, but Ted shook his head.

"Where is your sunbonnet, Pen? You could rip the lining and put it in and they'd never find it," he suggested eagerly. "Run up to the house and fix it, and see if you can't manage to get some bread, too, and a blanket. You know mother planned to walk to the village this afternoon."

"Mayn't I write a note and just say 'Don't worry'?" asked Penny.

"Yes, but not a word more. Remember, not a word more," said Ted, and Penny ran swiftly toward the house.

There was no sign of her mother, and the little girl found the door-key under the door-step, where it was always concealed when all the family were absent; she unlocked the door and entered. Speeding up the stairs she pulled a gray woolen blanket from the bed; then she pulled the homespun trousers from their hiding place and rolled them in the blanket and hurried back to the kitchen. She saw Ted's coat hanging beside her sunbonnet, and that too was rolled up in the blanket together with a loaf of bread, a tin cup and some squares of molasses gingerbread.

Penny now hunted through her mother's work-basket for scissors, thread and needle. She ripped the lining of her sunbonnet and carefully slipped the blue letter in between the lining and the outside. Then she sewed up the opening as neatly as possible, and was just putting the sunbonnet on when she heard steps, and looked up with frightened eyes, wondering if it would be her mother or Squire Dickinson. But it was Ted.

"You're awfully slow," he exclaimed. "Is this the blanket? Come on. I saw mother; she'll be here in five minutes," and he grabbed the bundle and fled toward the shore. But Penny found a bit of paper and her mother's pencil and wrote: "Don't worry," and fastened it to the case of the clock; then she too ran swiftly across the field, and when Mrs. Balfour reached her gate she saw Ted's boat sailing out toward Prudence Island.

CHAPTER V

THE BLUE SUNBONNET

"I WONDER where those children are off to now," Mrs. Balfour said to herself with a little smile as she read Penny's "Don't worry." "They will probably be late to supper. They are good, thoughtful children," she added, looking at the little scrap of paper. But, when the hour for supper came, Mrs. Balfour was surprised to find that her loaf of bread had vanished, and that the freshly baked gingerbread had disappeared. "My soul!" she exclaimed, looking into the empty jars as if unable to believe in their emptiness. Then she looked about the kitchen. What was her work-basket doing there, with its contents in such disorder? She picked up the scissors, and set the basket back on the little stand under the clock, resolving to speak very firmly to Ted and Penny on their return. "Late afternoon is no time for them to start off for a picnic," she said aloud as she started up the kitchen fire, and began to mix up a "johnny-cake" of coarse corn meal, resolving to herself that she would make no more gingerbread for a week to come as a visible sign of her displeasure.

As the twilight deepened Mrs. Balfour drove the cows up from the field, took care of the milk, and did the chores which Ted always took so much pride in doing. It was the last day of June, and the day lingered, so that when everything was finished it was still light, and Mrs. Balfour decided to climb Bayberry Hill, having no doubt that she would see the little "Modeerf" coming swiftly toward land. But there was no boat to be seen on the calm waters of the bay. A little breeze from the land brought the fragrance of many growing and blossoming things, and as the evening stars began to show in the pale sky it would have seemed a picture of peaceful beauty had it not been for the shadow of the dark war-ships in the distance.

"Don't worry." Mrs. Balfour repeated Penelope's written message as she walked back to the house, and tried to assure herself that her children were safe. When she found the blanket missing from Penny's bed, evidently hastily pulled off, she stared in amazement and a new fear entered her heart.

"My soul!" she exclaimed. "I do believe those children have started off to try and see their father! 'Don't worry,'" she repeated to herself. "Well, I guess I must try not to. I must be sure that their Heavenly Father will care for them."

By morning Mrs. Balfour had made up her mind to say nothing to the Dickinsons of the way in which Ted and Penny had left home. She was busy with the morning's work when she heard someone say: "Good-morning, Mistress Balfour. Where's Penny?" and she looked around to see Florence standing on the door-step.

"Come right in, Florence," and Mrs. Balfour smiled at the little figure in its spotless white dress and fresh sunbonnet; and then the thought of her own little girl made her face grow very sober.

"Where's Penny?" repeated Florence, coming into the pleasant room.

"Penny and Ted have both gone away in the boat," replied Mrs. Balfour.

"Gone away?" questioned Florence with startled eyes.

"They have gone sailing," answered Mrs. Balfour, "and I am going up on Bayberry Hill to get bayberries for more candles. You can come, too, and perhaps we shall see the boat."

"I can stay until noon," replied Florence; "perhaps they will come sailing in before that time; and if we see them from Bayberry Hill may I not go to the cove to meet them?"

"Yes, indeed; we will both go," responded Mrs. Balfour, who was very glad of the little girl's company, for it was very hard for her to obey Penelope's written message not to worry when she thought of her children spending the night in an open boat, or perhaps taken on board one of the strange vessels. She knew that Ted was a good sailor, and Penny well used to a boat, and she had little fear of accident, but she was afraid of the Tory soldiers.

"My grandfather told me to ask Ted if he saw a blue letter in the boat?" continued Florence.

"A blue letter?" exclaimed Mrs. Balfour.

"Yes," said the little girl. "Grandpa says if Ted did not find the letter that he must have thrown two on board the war-ship."

Mrs. Balfour's breath came quickly. She understood now what had sent Ted and Penny off without a word to her of their errand.

"Was it a letter of importance?" she asked.

"Grandpa didn't say," responded Florence. "I don't believe it was, for grandpa laughed and said the English captain would think he was a postman."

Nothing more was said about the letter, but Mrs. Balfour's eyes no longer searched the harbor for a sight of Ted's boat. If the children had started for the American camp at Tiverton, carrying with them, as Mrs. Balfour now thought possible, a letter of importance, who knew what might befall them, or when they would return home? She was now seriously alarmed for their safety, and realized that if the squire knew that Ted and Penny had not been at home since the previous day he would at once guess the truth and that they would all be in greater danger than ever. "He might even have me arrested as a spy," she thought fearfully. For it was a time when neighborly duties and friendship were set aside easily, and the squire would not forgive Ted and Penny if he discovered what they had done.

"There comes grandpa to take me home," said Florence, as they came down the hill. The squire greeted Mrs. Balfour pleasantly as he came to meet them, and asked politely as to his neighbor's health.

"And where are your young people this morning?" he inquired.

"They are out sailing," declared Florence, before Mrs. Balfour could answer, "and Ted did not find a blue letter, did he, Mrs. Balfour?"

"I do not know," Mrs. Balfour managed to answer, not looking at the squire.

"Of no consequence; an order for groceries," said the squire.

"Do you send your letters by English war-ships, Squire Dickinson?" Mrs. Balfour asked, with a little touch of scorn in her voice.

"The only safe way," answered the squire. "Your son is a fine sailor, Mrs. Balfour. He ran the 'Modeerf' so near the ship that I was able to greet the King's loyal sailors. Come, Florence," and with another polite bow, Squire Dickinson took Florence's hand and they started for Stone House, while Mrs. Balfour entered her own home, resolved to trust that the wisdom greater than her own would protect and bring her children safely home.

At the very hour when Florence and the squire were walking through the pine woods Penny and Ted were sitting behind a big rock on the Tiverton shore eating the last crumbs of the loaf of bread. The gingerbread had been eaten for their supper the night before.

"I don't believe anybody would notice the 'Modeerf' unless they were trying to hide a boat themselves," said Ted, a little anxiously, as he peered down at the rocky shore where they had landed the night before. A fair wind had favored them until they passed Prudence Island and Cannon Point, and then Ted had rowed the boat to the shore where they were now eating their dry bread and thinking, with a feeling of homesickness, of the warm porridge and milk at home.

The night had been warm and starlit, and Penny and Ted had slept soundly on a bed of moss, behind this big rock, not far from the shore. Ted had been glad of his coat, leaving the blanket for Penny.

"What on earth did you bring these old things for?" he asked, when he discovered his old trousers.

"Well, Ted Balfour! Didn't you say that it would be a lot easier for us to visit father if it wasn't for my being a girl and wearing girls' clothes?" responded Penny in an injured tone. "And I was going to wear your clothes, and cut off my braid so as to be as much like a boy as I could."

"Don't you do it!" exclaimed Ted. "Why, if you weren't wearing a sunbonnet I don't know what would happen to us. A boy would look pretty in a sunbonnet, wouldn't he?"

"Nobody looks pretty in a sunbonnet," said Penny despondently, "and sleeping in one is dreadful," for Ted had insisted that Penny should not remove the blue sunbonnet for even a moment; and its gingham strings were tied in a series of knots that Penny was perfectly sure could never be untied.

The brother and sister did not know where the American camp was, but Ted was sure that he could find it; and when they had finished the bread Penny rolled up the cup, trousers and blanket, which she insisted on carrying, Ted swung his jacket over his shoulders and, with a last look at the little boat, they started along the shore in the direction in which they thought the camp was located.

For a time they followed the shore, and then made their way up the bank and across a rough pasture, and from here they could see the white tents of the American camp.

"We can get there by noon," exclaimed Penny joyfully, "and they will give us something to eat. I'm awfully hungry."

"Now, Penny, I tell you what I think we'd better do," said Ted. "I had better not go to camp with you. I'm a boy, and I had better go first and find father and tell him; and then we'll come and get your sunbonnet. Perhaps it wouldn't be right for a girl to go marching into camp!" and Ted tried to look very serious and superior.

"My sunbonnet!" exclaimed Penny, tying another knot in the gingham strings. "Well, Ted Balfour, my sunbonnet shan't go one step without me. I want to see my father, and I want to see Colonel William Barton. And after making me wear the horrid thing all night," and one more knot was added swiftly to the others.

"Stop tying knots in those strings, Pen; I'll have to cut it off if you keep on," said Ted. "Come on ; we'll go a little nearer, anyway. But I think you ought to do as I say, Pen."

"Why?" Penny asked. "I found the letter, didn't I? And I sewed it into this hateful old sunbonnet ——"

"Hush!" warned Ted. "There's a man——" But before he could say more, a man, brown as an Indian, bareheaded, and wearing clothes so old that Ted wondered how they held together, rose up from behind a clump of blossoming laurel where he had evidently been sleeping, and where he must have heard all that the brother and sister had said.

"So the letter is sewed into the sunbonnet, is it?" he asked, smiling down at the two surprised and frightened children. "Well, I call that a first-rate plan. Whose letter is it?"

"Squire Dickinson's," faltered Penny, and as she saw Ted's scowl, she realized that she ought not to have answered the question. At the answer the man's face changed, and for a moment he did not speak. Then he said, "And so you are taking the squire's letter to a friend of his, I suppose?"

This time Penny kept silent, but Ted answered, "I guess you heard us say that we were going to the American camp to see our father."

"So I did! Why, so I did," agreed the man, watching the boy's face sharply. "I suppose you are both good Tory children?"

Ted and Penny looked fearfully at each other. Penny was afraid to speak at all, and Ted was sure that this man was a Tory spy, and would not speak.

"Off with You"

"I see. Of course you must be, or Squire Dickinson would not trust his letters to you. What is your father's name?" demanded the man, who was now unsheathing a knife from his leather belt.

Neither of the frightened children responded.

"'Tis a poor business to send children on such an errand, even if their father is a Tory spy," whispered the man to himself. "Well, I'll not urge you to tell. I can find out," he continued. "Now, as your bonnet strings are so well tied 'twill be easier to cut them," and with a careful stroke of his knife he cut the gingham strings of Penny's sunbonnet and stood holding it in his hand. "Now," he said, "you youngsters go back to the squire, and tell him that his letter is in good hands. Off with you!" and his look was so threatening that both Ted and Penny turned and ran toward the shore.

The man, holding the blue sunbonnet, watched them out of sight. Then he turned and moved swiftly toward the American camp. "A good morning's work," he said to himself. "These must be the children of some Tory spy in Colonel Barton's camp, bringing news." For this man was himself a picket of the American camp, and little knew that Ted and Penny were as loyal as himself. He blamed himself for being too tender-hearted in letting the children go free; but he lost no time in carrying the blue sunbonnet to Colonel William Barton, and explaining how it had come into his possession.

CHAPTER VI

THE WRONG VERSE

PENNY could feel the tears running down her cheeks as she fled across the pasture, and scrambled down to the rocky shore. Ted was just ahead of her, and neither of the children spoke until they were again close to the "Modeerf."

"It was all my fault! I just told that Tory all our plan," sobbed Penny, as she stowed the rolled up blanket under the front seat, and took her usual place in the boat. Ted did not answer; he, too, felt that it was all Penny's fault, "talking all about her silly sunbonnet," and he made ready in silence for their homeward voyage. As the sail caught the wind, and the boat shot out from its safe harbor behind the rocks, Penny spoke again.

"I s'pose you wish I hadn't come," she said.

"Never mind, Pen," Ted responded; "but I don't see what that man was doing so near the American camp. But the Tories are everywhere."

Penelope's face brightened. If Ted was not going to scold, she could bear with better courage the terrible disappointment of not seeing her father and Colonel Barton's camp.

"I wish we had opened the letter and read it," declared Ted, as the boat rounded Hog Island, and headed straight toward home.

"Theodore Balfour!" exclaimed Penny; for the Balfour children had been taught that to open, or to read, a letter intended for another person was an act of dishonesty.

"Well, I do!" repeated Ted. "Reading a letter like that is different. If I knew what was in it, I could have managed to reach the American camp and told it to father."

But Penny shook her head, although she resolved to ask her mother if one had to be just as honest with the people with whom their country was at war as with other people.

Mrs. Balfour saw the little boat rounding the point and hastened to the shore, her heart filled with thankfulness.

"Hello, mother!" Ted shouted, and Penny waved.

"Just think, Ted, we haven't had much to eat since yesterday noon," Penny said, as they came near the landing place.

"Don't say a word to mother about anything until we are in the house, Pen," warned Ted, as he swung the "Modeerf" alongside of the flat rock where, at high tide, they could step ashore.

"Oh, mother!" exclaimed Penny joyfully, as her mother's eager arms clasped her close. "You look just the same!"

This made both Mrs. Balfour and Ted laugh heartily, for Penelope's voice sounded as if she had returned from a far journey of many months.

Penny laughed too, as she stood with her mother's arm about her waiting for Ted to unship the mast, and leave the boat in its usual order.

"Children, no one knows that you were away last night. I thought it best not to tell the squire," said Mrs. Balfour as they walked toward home.

"Good for you, mother!" exclaimed Ted. "I knew you would make everything all right," and he looked at his mother with admiring eyes.

"It was all horrid," Penelope began. "I wore my sunbonnet all night, and——"

"Pen!" came Ted's warning voice, and Penny's hand went quickly to her mouth, and not another word did she speak until they had reached the shelter of the little house.

Ted threw the bundle of blanket and clothing on the kitchen floor, and ran to the spring-house for a bucket of fresh water.

"Mother, may I talk now?" Penny asked eagerly.

"Not yet, dear," responded Mrs. Balfour. "Run upstairs and change all your things. I'll bring you up some warm water, and as soon as you are ready we will have dinner."

"But it is almost supper-time," responded Penny, picking up the bundle and tugging it toward the stairs. "But I am hungry enough to eat dinner and supper at once."

Penny was glad to bathe her tired feet in the warm water, and to put on the freshly ironed gingham dress. Then, when her hair was well brushed and rebraided, she hurried back to the kitchen. Ted, who usually wore moccasins, was now barefooted, and his yellow hair was still damp from its recent plunge into a basin of cold water.

As Mrs. Balfour set the platter of steaming cream toast on the table, the dish of scrambled eggs, and a tumbler filled with jelly, Penny and Ted both exclaimed joyfully, and as they took their usual seats at the table, Mrs. Balfour smiled at their eagerness; but there was a little mist before her eyes, for she was thinking of the many unhappy accidents that might have befallen the children, who were now safe at home.

As their mother filled their plates Ted began the story of their adventure. Penny did not speak. Glad as she was to be safe with her dear mother, the little girl was sure that she had been the cause of their failure to deliver the letter to her father; and she was resolving to herself that she must, in some way, undo the harm she had done. Just how this could be done Penny did not know, but her thoughts were very busy.

When she went up-stairs that night Penny unrolled the blanket, folded it neatly and laid it on a chair. For her mother had said that it must be washed before it could again be put on the bed. The tin cup was lost, and Penny wondered if it were near the big rock on Tiverton shore, where they had slept the previous night.

Penny hid the old trousers again, for she was thinking to herself that she might even yet start off, and that it might be safer to wear boys' clothes than girls'.

When Penny opened her eyes the next morning she remembered that it was Sunday. There would be no sailing to-day, nor could Florence come over for her daily visit. Penny was rather glad of this, as she lay half-awake in the comfortable bed wondering if her mother would expect her to go to Sunday-school as usual; and as Penny lay thinking of this she remembered that she had not learned a verse from the Bible, for every member of the Sunday-school was expected to recite a verse.

"You can't sleep any longer, children, or you will be late for Sunday-school," called Mrs. Balfour. The Sunday-school was held before the morning service in the white church at Warwick Village, a mile distant from the Balfour farm.

Ted and Penny had little time to spare. They ate their porridge and milk, and started briskly off toward the church. Mrs. Balfour watched them until the turn of the road hid them from her sight, and was quite sure that none of the children in the Warwick meeting house would be better behaved than Theodore and Penelope. But she sighed a little as she remembered that Penny must wear her gingham dress to meeting, and that Ted's only boots, in spite of their fine coat of grease, were worn and scrubby.

But neither Ted nor his sister was thinking of clothes as they walked along the pleasant country road, which crept up a little hill from which they could plainly see the British war vessel, to whose sailors the squire had called his greeting.

"She's getting up sail!" Ted exclaimed. "Look, Pen. Those Tories care no more for the Sabbath than for any other day," cried the young Puritan.

"I'm glad they're going, Sunday or no Sunday," responded Penny; "then the squire won't find out——"

"Pen!" Ted's quick exclamation interrupted her, and Penny looked quickly behind her, half expecting to see the squire himself.

"Well, you know what I mean, Ted Balfour," she concluded.

"Yes, I do, but I should think you'd had a lesson not to talk anywheres about anything," responded Ted.

Penny felt that, much as she deserved reproof, this was rather severe discipline; but she closed her lips firmly resolved not to speak again until they reached the meeting-house.

"The British vessel is going down the harbor toward Newport," Ted said; "but come on, Pen, we must hurry."

Ted did not feel much like talking himself, and did not notice Penny's silence. They reached the meeting-house in good season, and slipped quietly into their seats; and suddenly Penny remembered that she had not learned a Bible verse, nor could she remember one; and this so troubled her that she could not follow the words of the prayer; and when she heard one after another rise and repeat the required verse, she felt her face growing crimson and her heart beating in fear. What should she do when her own name was called? And at that moment her doom sounded, "Penelope Balfour!" To the little girl the voice seemed to come from a long way off.

"Say your verse, dear child," whispered a kind woman from the seat behind her. "Stand up and say your verse," and Penny found herself standing. She must say a verse. She shut her eyes tight.

"Prudence, Patience, Hope and Despair,
    And little Hog Island, right over there,"

repeated Penny, and sank back into her seat, her eyes still shut tight. She wondered if she would ever dare to open them upon an insulted world. There was a moment's dreadful silence; a faint titter sounded from a rear seat. Then Penny heard the name of another little girl called; and heard a faint voice murmur, "Be ye also perfect, even as your Father in heaven is perfect!"

"Perfect!" thought Penny, who believed herself an outlaw.

Just then she felt a friendly pat upon her folded hands, and ventured to look up. The minister's wife was sitting close beside her. And now Penny felt the kind hand close over her own, and give it a friendly squeeze. Of course the minister's wife could not whisper in Sunday-school, thought Penny, with a sense of consolation in the touch of the cool hand; and then the unbelievable happened! The minister's wife whispered!

"There is no harm in the verse, dear child," came the kind voice, and Penny drew a little nearer to this true friend, wondering to herself if it might not be possible to walk out from the meeting-house under this safe protection.

The long session dragged itself to an end, and gradually Penny's breath came naturally, and her fear and shame began to grow less. But Penny's thoughts were full of the dreadful ordeal of walking down the aisle to the door, and of meeting Ted. She was in the midst of these unhappy thoughts when she realized that the minister's wife had tightened her clasp on her hand, and was saying gently: "Come, Penelope," and in another moment Penny was walking toward the door, keeping very close to her friend's skirts.

When Ted had heard Penny's voice reciting the verse naming the well-known islands of Narragansett Bay he had been almost as terrified as Penny herself; and then, hearing the half-suppressed titters, and noticing the horrified expression on the faces of the older people, he became ashamed. His face grew very red, and he was very angry at his sister.

"She can go home alone," he vowed to himself, thinking that he would hurry from the church and go home across lots. Then he looked across the room at Penny, for in the Sunday-school the boys were on one side of the room and the girls on the other. She was looking down, and as Ted's eyes rested upon her he forgot all about being angry or ashamed because she had recited the wrong verse. He could only remember how bravely she had come to his rescue when he must have drowned but for her help. And he suddenly remembered his name for her, "Smiling Sally," because she was always so ready to smile and be happy. And Ted made at that moment a resolve which he never afterward forgot—a resolve that, no matter what happened, he would stand by Penny; and when the little girl reached the church door her brother stood there waiting for her, and even smiled at her.

The minister's wife looked at him approvingly, and bent over and kissed Penny's cheek as she said good-bye.

"I am coming over to see your mother one day this week, and ask her to let you make me a visit, dear child," she said, and stood watching Ted and Penny as they started, hand in hand, for home.

"Theodore Balfour will make a fine man," she prophesied, as she turned back to the church.

CHAPTER VII

FLORENCE TELLS A SECRET

"I DON'T know what made me say that verse," said Penelope, as Ted released her hand from his firm clasp.

"I do!" responded Ted. "You thought you must say something, and that was the only verse you could remember. 'Tis a good verse. It does but repeat the names of the islands. There is no harm in it."

Penny now looked at Ted, and there was a more hopeful expression in her blue eyes. "The minister's wife said those very words, Ted," she said, "but I know the girls and boys were all laughing at me."

"Let 'em laugh," declared Ted. "I'll bet there's not a girl in that Sunday-school who can swim as well as you can."

Penny was now her own smiling self again. With the minister's wife for her friend, and with Ted as her champion she was no longer afraid, although she was still sorry and ashamed and said again, "I don't know what made me say it." But it was in a very different voice from her former declaration.

The brother and sister now began to talk of the Tory, as they still believed him to be, who had taken the squire's letter from them. They talked in low voices, and now and then stopped to look cautiously around and listen; for both the children feared to speak aloud of their adventure.

"Mother talked to me about it this morning," said Ted, "and she says that perhaps the man was an American soldier who thought we were Tories; but I don't think he was." There was a question in the boy's tone, as if he almost hoped that Penny would agree with their mother. But Penny made no response, and Ted continued: "Mother made me promise that I would never start off for the American camp, or on any other trip, without talking it over with her. So I can't do anything to help now, for mother wouldn't let me go again."

"You help all the time, Ted," declared Penny. "Mother says that if it weren't for the work the boys and girls do on the farms and in the houses, our soldiers would have nothing to eat or wear."

"There comes the squire!" exclaimed Ted, and drew Penny out of the road for the carriage to pass. It was a wide-seated chaise on high springs, with a small, high seat in front for the driver, where Black Aleck held the reins.

The squire, Florence and her mother were in the chaise, and Florence waved her hand, and called out a greeting as the chaise swung by.

"I wish we didn't live neighbors to the Dickinsons," grumbled Ted, as he and Penny walked on.

"Why?" questioned the little girl.

"Because it makes me feel mean all the time. I hate Tories, and the squire's the rankest Tory on this side of the shore, but if he wasn't a Tory I'd like him first-rate, even if he did try to make me help the old British," said Ted.

When they reached home Mrs. Balfour listened to Penny's account of her sad adventure in Sunday-school, and quite agreed with Ted and the minister's wife that it was not the dreadful sin Penny had feared it to be.

"When I got started I had to say it all," explained Penny. "I couldn't stop. Mother, if the minister's wife really invites me to make her a visit may I go?"

"Yes, indeed!" responded Mrs. Balfour; "it will be a great honor for a little girl to visit the minister's wife; and she is indeed kind to ask you." And Mrs. Balfour thought to herself that she would not refuse the minister's wife the pleasure of a visit, should she really ask it, from her little Penelope. For there were no children in the minister's family, and Mrs. Balfour often thought that Mrs. Godfrey must sometimes envy her the possession of Ted and Penny.

The remainder of the day passed quietly. After dinner Mrs. Balfour and the children went to the seat under the big oak tree.

"Pen forgot all about wanting to stop at Drum Rock to-day," said Ted, as they walked across the field to the tree.

Drum Rock, a curious boulder, so held in the hollow of its stony bed that it could be rocked without overturning, was a natural curiosity of that part of the Narragansett shore. It was about half-way between the Balfour farm and the church, in a thick growth of spruce, and hard to find unless one were familiar with its location. Usually Penny insisted on leaving the road on their way home from church to visit Drum Rock; but to-day she had not even thought of it. This rocking stone was used by the Indians as a signal of danger, as it formerly made a deep bell-like sound that could be heard for a considerable distance.

Sunday afternoons always seemed the most pleasant part of the week to Ted and Penny; for then their father and mother planned some special treat for the children. Before Mr. Balfour had joined the army, he would often take them on some pleasant walk. In winter they would gather around the open fire, and he would tell them stories of the early days of Narragansett Colony, when the red men roamed the forests, or built their camps in the clearings. For Penny the happiest hour of the whole week was the Sunday night supper. For, since she was eight years old, it was Penny who prepared this simple meal. She stirred up and baked the johnny-cake of Indian meal; she baked the potatoes, and now and then made the spice cakes which all the family praised and enjoyed. It was a time when people were satisfied with simple and homely fare; but the Balfours were sure that their Sunday night supper was all any one could ask.

As the little family sat under the big oak tree this Sunday afternoon their thoughts were with the absent father, and, after Ted spoke of Drum Rock, Penelope said:

"Mother, tell us about King Philip."

Other Indian leaders had been called sachem, or chief, but this red man was always known as King; and Penny never tired of hearing of him, and of Massasoit, that friendly sachem to whom the white settlers owed so much, although Philip forgot the peaceful precepts of his father.

"Begin where King Philip left Massachusetts and made a fort on the island in the big swamp where he thought no white man could reach him," suggested Ted.

So Mrs. Balfour repeated the story of the beleaguered Indians, led by King Philip, and hunted from one fastness to another, and of Philip's returning by stealth to his own home, Pocanoket, not many miles from the Balfour farm. His fortress and storehouse in the great swamp were betrayed by one of his followers, a renegade Indian, who, hidden by a December snowstorm and finding solid ice upon which it was possible to cross the swamp, guided a large force of settlers to the camp, so that Philip's followers were conquered and many of them destroyed.

"Those were dreadful times," said Mrs. Balfour, as she finished the story.

"Not much worse than these," declared Ted, springing to his feet. "I heard at the church that loyal men were going to drive every Tory from the Colony."

But Mrs. Balfour would not talk of Tories or of "loyal men." And Penny was sure that it was time to prepare supper.

"Ted and I will sit here until we are called to supper," said Mrs. Balfour smilingly, as Penny ran toward the house.

Ted had laid the fire ready to light, and in a few minutes Penny had carefully sifted the Indian meal into the mixing-bowl and, with her apron covering her clean cotton dress, was stirring in the right proportion of milk and water, when she heard her name called from the kitchen door.

"Penny!" called the voice, and Penny turned quickly to find Florence standing smiling at her from the kitchen doorway. "Penny, do you want me to stay to supper?" she asked. "I told mother you wanted me, and she said I might. You do want me, don't you, Pen?" and there was a pleading note in the little girl's voice.

"Yes, it's nice to have company," replied Penny, "and you can help get supper." Penny was sure that no one could be more kind to a guest than to bestow such a privilege, and Florence's face beamed with satisfaction.

"Truly?" she responded, as if she could hardly believe in her good fortune.

Penny stopped stirring the johnny-cake, and looked sharply at her little visitor, then shook her head. "I didn't notice your clothes, Florence, when I said that you could help," she said.

"What's the matter with my clothes?" and Florence looked anxiously down at the dainty dress of blue muslin, with its ruffles edged with delicate lace, and at the broad sash of blue silk.

"They are too good," declared Penny, and she looked at the pretty muslin disapprovingly. "I shouldn't think you would ever have a bit of fun, Florence; not a single bit," she continued, "for there isn't a minute of the day that you're not all dressed up."

Florence seated herself on one of the wooden kitchen chairs, and replied despondently, "I don't have much fun. Do you suppose it's because I have such pretty dresses?"

"That's one reason," said Penny, thinking to herself that of course a girl whose father was a Tory couldn't expect to be very happy.

"Penny, let me help," pleaded Florence, "just this once; because—because—" and to Penny's amazement Florence put her hands over her face and began to cry.

"Stop crying, Florence!" commanded Penny. "Of course I'll let you help. I was only thinking about your clothes. You can set the table if you want to; and," she continued as Florence's sobs continued, "you can wash the potatoes and put them in the oven."

At this generous offer Florence wiped her eyes with a tiny handkerchief, and responded: "I wasn't crying about not helping, and I wasn't crying about my clothes. I was crying about something dreadful. It's a secret," and she looked at Penny hopefully. For a secret, to Florence, was a gift to bestow after due persuasion.

But Penny was now turning the golden mixture of her corn-cake into its baking tin, and made no answer.

"It's a secret," repeated Florence, sliding down from the chair, and coming close to Penny.

"The potatoes are in a basket in the shed," said Penny. "You take that little tin pan and bring in six. Pick out small ones. And there's mother's apron; you tie it around your neck."

"I don't want any apron," declared Florence, taking the small pan and starting for the shed. "I don't care what happens to my clothes."

"Well, you ought to care," Penny called, thinking to herself that if Florence had only two well-worn cotton dresses she would not be so scornful of pretty muslins. And Penelope sighed a little, for she often wished that she could have one pretty dress, just one.

"Don't you want to hear my secret?" asked Florence, coming in from the shed, and stumbling over the long apron.

"But you can't tell a secret," said Penny; "secrets are never to be told."

"I don't care," pouted Florence. "I'm going to tell you, even if grandpa said it was a secret. It's dreadful, Penny!" and Florence looked quite ready to cry again.

"I'll wash those potatoes," said Penny; "the oven's just right," and she took the pan from Florence, looked at its contents and began to laugh. "Oh, Florence! Don't you know a potato when you see it? These are turnips."

"Penny, listen!" and Florence grasped Penny's arm and spoke rapidly. "Grandfather is going to run away. Yes, he is. To Boston; and he's going to take us all with him. We're going to-morrow night!"

The pan fell from Penny's grasp, and the turnips rolled over the clean floor.

"What is he going to run away for?" gasped Penny.

Florence shook her head. "I don't know, Penny; but isn't it dreadful? Perhaps I shan't ever see you again," and Florence began to cry.

Penelope put her arms about her little friend, almost ready to cry herself, and quite forgetting that Florence had committed so grave a fault as betraying a secret. She entirely forgot the johnny-cake in the hot oven, and that it was time for supper as she stood trying to comfort Florence, and asking eager questions about the squire's plans.

"We are going in the coach, all of us," Florence said. "Black Aleck is going to drive, and Hitty and Jane are going too. Grandpa says we may get to Boston and we may not."

"Why, children! What is the matter?" and Mrs. Balfour stepped into the room, and looked at the two little girls. "And what are these turnips doing on the floor? And what's burning?" and Mrs. Balfour sniffed and looked toward the brick oven.

"My johnny-cake!" exclaimed Penny, quite forgetting Florence.

Mrs. Balfour picked up the turnips, and said kindly, "Don't cry, Florence; dropping a pan of turnips is nothing to cry about."

"Penny dropped the pan," faltered Florence, who began to wish that she had not betrayed her grandfather's secret. Perhaps Penny would tell Mrs. Balfour, she thought, and then all sorts of things might happen; for Florence now remembered that the Balfours were rebels, and that her grandfather's flight had something to do with rebels. She ran after Penny. "You mustn't tell. Promise you won't!" she whispered.

"I won't tell," Penny promised, "but my johnny-cake is burned to a crisp," and Penny thought to herself that she wished Florence had waited until after supper before telling the secret.

"We shall have to do without hot corn-cake to-night," Mrs. Balfour said; and when Ted suggested bread and milk, Penelope agreed eagerly, for she could think only of what Florence had told her.

Both the little girls were very quiet at supper, and as soon as they had finished their bread and milk Penny asked if she might not walk toward Stone House with Florence, and Mrs. Balfour gave her permission.

"What's the matter with Florence?" Ted asked his mother, as the two little girls started.

"I can't imagine," replied Mrs. Balfour. "She was crying when I came in."

"Wanted to get supper, perhaps, and Pen wouldn't let her," answered Ted laughingly.

CHAPTER VIII

GIFTS

FLORENCE held close to Penny's hand as they walked across the field. Florence was an only child, and Penny was the only little girl whom she knew well. Now and then Florence had visited with her mother at the home of some other wealthy Tory where there were children of her own age; but she never felt really acquainted with those children, and her happiest hours were those spent with Penelope and Ted. It seemed a very strange and unhappy plan to Florence to leave Stone House and the Balfours. Even the thought that she would soon see her father did little to comfort her.

"What makes your grandpa start in the night?" asked Penny.

"I heard him tell mother that we must start before the rebels took our horses, and that 'twas safer to go without being seen," answered Florence.

"Rebels don't take horses that don't belong to them. That's Tories' work," said Penny.

"All I know is what grandpa said," responded Florence in so humble a manner that Penny clasped her hand more closely, and said kindly:

"It's not your fault, Florence."

"Grandpa said that, now the British ship had gone down to Newport, he no longer felt safe. He said the rebels taunted him when he drove through Warwick Village."

This seemed rather dreadful to Penny, though she was quite sure that Tories could never be in the right.

"I don't suppose I'll ever come back," went on Florence, "and you will forget all about me, Penny."

"I couldn't!" responded Penelope. "You know I couldn't forget you, Florence. And when everything is all settled right, you will come back to Stone House, and father will come home and we shall all be happy."

"But it isn't going to be settled right, never! Grandpa says so. He says that it looks as if the Americans would win!"

Penny stopped short, and drew her hand from Florence's clasp.

"They ought to win. America doesn't want a king!" she declared.

"Oh, Penny!" and Florence was again ready to weep. "I don't care, anyway. All I feel bad about is leaving you. And I haven't told you the worst. We're going to England."

Penny was now as surprised and troubled as Florence could wish. If the Dickinsons sailed away to that far-off place, it was indeed unlikely that she would ever see Florence again, and Penny quickly realized that not to see Florence would make a very great difference to her, and for a moment she did not speak.

"And, Penny, I'm going to give you something to remember me by. Something you can always keep," said Florence. "You'll take it, won't you?"

Penny nodded. She was afraid that if Florence said another word she would cry, and Penny did not believe in crying.

"I am going to bring it to you to-morrow," said Florence, "and you will always keep it, won't you, Penny?"

Penny nodded again, but her warm clasp of Florence's hand was all the promise Florence wanted.

"Can't you come and stay all day to-morrow, Florence?" asked Penny when they had reached the stone wall that separated the grounds of Stone House from the Balfour field.

"Yes, Penny, I am sure I can, for I heard mother say that to-morrow every one must be up early, and that it would be a busy day. So when I tell her that you have invited me to stay all day, I know she'll say yes," and Florence smiled happily at the thought of the pleasure of a whole day at Balfour farm.

The little girls were now sitting on the top of the low stone wall. They could see the highway, and Stone House with its gardens and terraces. As they sat talking happily of what they would do on the morrow, they nearly forgot that after the morrow Florence would be far away.

"There comes Hitty after me," exclaimed Florence, scrambling hastily down on the further side of the wall. "I'll come early. Good-night, dear Pen!"

"Good-night, dear Florence," responded Penelope.

As she walked slowly toward home she wondered why Florence had said "Dear Pen," and why she had responded "Dear Florence"; and she remembered how often they had disagreed and parted in anger; and Penny's face was very sober and she wished with all her heart that she had always been kind to her little friend.

When the child went to bed that night she lay long awake thinking of the journey on which Florence was so soon to start, and of the gift Florence would bring on the next day. Penny thought over her own few possessions for some remembrance for Florence.

"I can't give her the gold acorn pin, for Grandma Balfour left me that in her will; and I can't give her my silver thimble, for my father gave it to me, and that's all I have, except my piece of money," thought Penelope as she lay watching the summer stars through the window. Then suddenly she remembered that her "piece of money," a gold sovereign, was her very own to do just as she pleased with. Her father had given it to her two years before, and Penny kept it safely in a little box of carved wood in the drawer of the light stand that stood near the head of her bed.

"I'll give that to Florence. Then she can always keep it to remember me," and now Penny was ready for sleep.

It was early when she awoke the next morning. She could hear a sleepy bird in its nest in the elm tree, giving a few half-hearted notes to the dawn, but no other sound.

"I'll start the fire," thought Pen gleefully, for both she and Ted were eager to help with the household

work; but it was usually Ted who was up first, and
Penny smiled as she tiptoed about her room thinking
that this morning she would surely be first. But as she
stepped into the little passageway there was Ted just
going down the stairs.

Ted looked at her in surprise. "You must have been
as still as a mouse," he said, "for I didn't hear a sound."

"Let's have breakfast all ready when mother comes
down," responded Penny. "And, Ted, Florence is coming early, to stay all day, and I want her to have the
nicest time she ever had. What can we do that she will
like best of anything?"

The brother and sister were standing in the kitchen,
and Ted exclaimed: "Well, Pen, I didn't know you
liked Florence's company so well. How long is it
since you were scolding because she was always coming over here? And now you've invited her to spend
the day, and afraid that she won't have a good time.
What's happened?"

"I've been mean to Florence," responded Penny.

"Girls are funny," declared Ted, "but you're all right,
'Smiling Sally'; I'll take you out sailing, if that's what
you want."

"Thank you, 'Sammy,'" said Penny, who sometimes
liked to call her brother by the name the English
sailors had given him.

"Well, what early birds!" exclaimed Mrs. Balfour,
coming into the kitchen, "and the porridge nearly
cooked, and the table set," and she smiled approving-

ly at her little daughter, and listened to Penelope's plans for the day.

"Mother, mayn't we all go on a picnic? Ted has promised to take us sailing. Won't you go with us? And can't we have a clambake?" asked Penny, holding out her bowl for a second helping of porridge.

"Who is going to dig the clams, Miss Pen?" asked Ted.

"I will!" replied Penny, meekly.

"Whatever is the matter with 'Smiling Sally' this morning!" exclaimed her brother. "Here she is up before the birds, gets breakfast, has really asked Florence to come, instead of running away when she sees her coming, and now is willing to dig clams!" and Ted waved his spoon as if it were a triumphant banner.

Mrs. Balfour wondered a little why Penny was so eager to plan a happy day for Florence, but said she was quite ready to go for a picnic, and thought a clambake would be the very best kind of picnic dinner. "And I don't believe that you will have to dig the clams either, Pen," she said.

"Of course she won't," laughed Ted, "but I'll have to work in the garden till dark if I loaf away the day," and with the air of a very busy man Ted hurried out to feed the hens, and look after his usual morning's work.

"I'll just stir up some spice cakes," said Mrs. Balfour, as Penny cleared the table. "But 'twill take the last of our molasses, and I do not know when we can get more," and an anxious look came into Mrs. Balfour's pleasant eyes.

The war was making the Colonies very poor; and especially along the shores of Narragansett Bay, where British ships blockaded the harbor, did the settlers feel the pinch of doing without many of the simple comforts of life. The little schooners with their cargoes of sugar and molasses could no longer bring supplies to the settlements; and the people had little money to pay the high prices for these articles when they were to be had.

But Penny was almost glad that the last of their precious store of molasses was to be used for Florence's pleasure; and when she saw her coming across the field Penny ran eagerly to meet her.

"We're going on a picnic to Warwick Neck," Penny called as she ran across the field, "and, oh, Florence, you look too nice for a picnic," she concluded, standing in front of her little guest and regarding her with admiring eyes.

Florence did indeed look too nice for the day's pleasure as Penny had planned it. Her white sunbonnet had an embroidered edge and flounce, her dress was white and heavily embroidered, and she wore white openworked knitted stockings. Everything the little girl wore had been the work of her Grandmother Dickinson.

"Penny, this is for you to wear always!" said Florence, unclasping a slender gold chain from her neck, and holding it out toward Penny. There was a tiny locket on the chain and on the locket was engraved "Florence." Penny looked at it admiringly. "You will keep it, won't you, Pen?" said Florence.

"Yes, always, Florence," responded Penny, in a very serious tone; and for a moment the two little girls stood silent, Penny holding the chain and locket in her hands.

"I'll clasp it 'round your neck, Penny," said Florence, and now the pretty locket swung over Pen's faded blue cotton dress.

With a quick motion the little girl pulled her dress over it. "Mother and Ted would ask about it," she explained in answer to Florence's questioning look. "To-morrow I'll tell them. And, Florence, I have a present for you, to keep always," and Penny drew from her pocket her treasured "piece of money," and slipped the gold coin into Florence's hand.

"Oh, Penny, I'll keep it forever. I'll wear it on a chain, just as you do the locket," and Florence now tied the coin in her handkerchief, and then poked the handkerchief under the top of her stocking.

The two little girls now walked toward the house, and both Mrs. Balfour and Ted told Florence that they were very glad to see her, and that the picnic was especially for her.

"It's funny," Ted whispered to his mother as they all walked toward the shore, "the way Pen and Florence keep hold of each other's hands. You'd think this was the last day they ever expected to see each other," and Ted, although he did not know it, had expressed just what Penny and Florence really believed.

CHAPTER IX

BROTHER JUNIPER

Ted headed the "Modeerf" toward a wooded point about a half-hour's sail distant.

"There's a little clearing under the big trees there," he explained to his mother, "and a good clam-bed on the shore." Ted had brought the wide-pronged clam digger, and a bucket to put the clams in, and there were potatoes to be baked in the hot ashes.

"I've never been to a clambake before," said Florence, as the little boat slid in between two long ledges, close to the shore, and Ted held the boat steady for his passengers to land.

"You must come with us again soon," responded Mrs. Balfour, and wondered why Florence should look so serious, and make no response to the invitation.

Ted made the boat fast, and led the way to the clearing he had spoken of. It was very near the shore, a pleasant grassy space, sheltered by the overhanging branches of big beech trees. There were clumps of fragrant bayberry bushes here and there, and the white blossoms of Solomon's Seal showed like tiny white stars along the border of the clearing.

Penny and Florence exclaimed delightedly, as they ran here and there, over the beauties of the place, and Mrs. Balfour said that it was just right for a clambake. For the clearing opened on the shore, and here the fire could be built to cook the potatoes and clams.

While Ted went off with his clam-fork and bucket to dig the clams Mrs. Balfour and the girls gathered rock-weed from the ledges, and sea-grass from the shore in which the clams were to be cooked. Now and then Penny would exclaim when some splash of sea-water fell on Florence's pretty dress; but as Florence only laughed Penny soon ceased to think about it. Both the little girls quite forgot their secret, and were as happy as Penny had wished they might be.

Ted was soon back, his bucket filled with white-shelled clams. "They are beauties!" he exclaimed, "and this ledge is just the right place for a fire."

Ted was well used to making out-of-door fires for cooking. First of all he scooped out a good-sized hole in the sand at the foot of the ledge and lined it with the sea-grass and rockweed. Then the clams were put in, well covered with rockweed. Over this Ted proceeded to pile on the light driftwood, and then lit his fire.

"Oh, Ted! You've forgotten your potatoes!" exclaimed Florence.

"Wait and see," laughed Ted.

"Ted isn't a 'Brother Juniper,'" said Mrs. Balfour, as they went back to the shady clearing to wait for the clams to cook. "Haven't you ever heard of Brother Juniper?" she asked, noticing the puzzled look on Florence's face.

"Who was he?" asked the little girl.

"He was a very good man who lived, many years ago, in a little town in Italy called Assisi," replied Mrs. Balfour. "He lived with other good men, and every day these 'Little Brothers,' as they called themselves, went about helping people, and giving all they could earn to people who needed it. They lived in a very small house, and one of the Brothers did the cooking.

"Brother Juniper thought that it was a pity to take so much time in getting food ready to eat, so when he was left in charge one day, a plan came into his head. He went about and got eggs and chickens and vegetables and meat. Then he made a big fire and borrowed a big iron pot; and all the time he sang happily, thinking to himself, 'I have found out the best way to cook; and I will cook all this food, and then 'twill last a week, and nobody will have to think about cooking for all that time.' So he hung the pot over the fire, and put in all the chickens, feathers and all, and the eggs in the shell, and the vegetables. Then he filled the pot with water, and soon it was boiling furiously. Well, when the others came in tired and hungry, Brother Juniper dished out some of the stew and brought it for them to eat. He told them what he had done, and that they would not have to do any cooking for a week. The Brothers sniffed at the stew, looked at him, and shook their heads. Not a mouthful did they eat, and Brother Juniper soon knew the reason. Then, because he had wasted so much good food, he did not eat a mouthful for several days. And that's why poor cooks are sometimes called Brother Juniper," concluded Mrs. Balfour.

It was a story that Ted and Penny had often heard, and they were surprised that Florence did not know it.

Ted replenished his fire, and in half an hour raked it from the top of the seaweed and took out the steaming clams into a tin pan they had brought for that purpose. The shells were opening, and the picnickers were quite ready to begin; but Ted was putting the potatoes into the hot sand, and raking the hot coals over the sand-covered oven.

"They will be all ready by the time we have eaten the clams," said Ted, and so they were. Then came the spice cakes; and with a drink of cool water from a spring that bubbled up very near the shore, their feast was complete.

Penny and Florence wandered about in the woods gathering big bunches of ferns and Solomon's Seal and laurel leaves.

"Mother will help us make some wreaths," said Penny, and this Mrs. Balfour was quite ready to do. She showed the little girls how to weave the glossy laurel leaves and white blossoms into beautiful wreaths.

"You can take one to your Grandmother Dickinson and one to your mother, Florence," Penny suggested as they finished the task.

Ted had put out the fire, and now came up and lay down on the grass near his mother.

"Tell us another story, mother," he asked.

"Shall I tell you a fable? About the larks and the farmer?" responded his mother.

Ted nodded, and Penny and Florence smiled happily at each other, for "a fable" was sure to be different and more interesting than a story.

"There was a brood of young larks in a field of corn," began Mrs. Balfour; "the corn was just ripe and ready to be gathered, and the mother lark, looking every day for the reapers, left word, whenever she left the nest in search of food, for the young larks to remember and tell her all the news they heard.

"One day, while she was absent, the farmer came to look at the state of the crops. 'It is full time,' said he, 'to call in all my neighbors and get my corn reaped.' When the mother lark came home, the young ones told her what they had heard, and begged her to find a new home for them at once. 'There is plenty of time for that,' said the mother lark; 'if he trusts to his neighbors there is no hurry; and his harvest will not be gathered to-day or to-morrow.'

"Next day, however, the farmer came again. The sun was even hotter, and the corn more ripe, and nothing done, and the farmer became very anxious. 'There is no time to lose,' he said to his son. 'We cannot wait for our neighbors; they have their own work to do. We must send at once for our relations. Hurry away and ask your uncles and cousins to come tomorrow and gather my corn.'

"The young larks were now in great fear, and told their mother what the farmer had said. 'Oh! if that is all,' said she, 'there is nothing to be afraid of, for the relations have their own harvest to attend to; but take great notice of what the farmer says next time, and be sure to tell me.' She went away early the next morning, and when the farmer came there was the grain dropping to the ground from over-ripeness, and no one to harvest it. He called his son. 'It is no use to wait longer,' he said, 'for either neighbors or relations; we must set to work ourselves without delay.'

"When the young larks told their mother this she said: 'Now it is indeed time to be off. For when a man takes up his work himself, instead of leaving it to others, then you may be sure the work will be done.'"

"That will be just the story to tell Hitty," laughed Florence. "She thinks a fable is really true."

"There is always a truth in it," responded Mrs. Balfour, "and we must remember to start home as soon as the tide turns."

"That's so," declared Ted, jumping up and running down to the shore, where a little creeping line of blue water showed that it was time for the "Modeerf" to head toward the Balfour shore.

"What is the matter with our sheep?" exclaimed Penny, as the boat came near the pasture slope.

Ted and Mrs. Balfour looked toward the hill pasture, and saw the sheep all running down the slope toward the shore. "There's a sloop close in," exclaimed Ted, "and there are men driving the sheep to the shore. It's the English. Oh, mother! Can't we make them let our sheep alone?"

"Oh, it's too bad," whispered Penny.

Mrs. Balfour made no response to Ted's question. There was nothing that they could do to recover the sheep. But Mrs. Balfour sighed as she remembered what the loss of them would mean, and wished, as she often did, that Colonel Waterman's regiment was not quartered so far from Balfour farm, and to wonder if after all she was not unwise in remaining at the farm while the war was going on.

Ted was furious that he could not prevent the men from taking the sheep. But Penny was only wishing that it had not happened that day.

"We were all so happy," she said, as they walked toward home.

"It was a lovely picnic. I never had such a good time!" declared Florence. "I'll never forget it, Pen. Never! And see, my dress is all spotted!" and Florence pointed to her dress as if the marks were another cause for delight.

It was now late in the afternoon, and Ted hurried off to attend to his work. Florence said Hitty was too busy to come for her, and Penny offered to walk as far as the wall; and now came the moment that Florence had so dreaded, when she must say good-bye to Mrs. Balfour. Tears came to the little girl's eyes when she looked into the face of her kind friend, and realized that she might never see her again.

"Good-bye, dear Mrs. Balfour," she said; and Mrs. Balfour stooped and kissed the sad little face, and said:

"Good-bye, dear child; you must come over whenever your mother is willing."

Without a word Florence turned and ran across the field, closely followed by Penelope. Mrs. Balfour had often seen Florence in tears; so, beyond a wandering thought as to what the present trouble might be, did not think much about it. "Perhaps Florence feels bad because Ted hurried off without a word of good-bye; or perhaps the child feels bad because our sheep have been taken," thought Mrs. Balfour. "She is a sensitive nature, poor child."

After Penny caught up with Florence the two girls walked slowly on together. Florence wiped her eyes, and now remembered that she had not bidden Ted good-bye. "You'll tell Ted good-bye for me, won't you, Penny?" she said.

"Yes," agreed Penny. "I'll tell him tomorrow after you're gone. He might think it funny if I told him to-night."

Penny's voice sounded almost too cheerful to Florence, and she choked back her sobs. "There'll be a surprise for you to-morrow, Penny, and a surprise for your mother and a surprise for Ted." And although Penny questioned earnestly, Florence would only shake her head and say, "Wait until to-morrow," and Penny became so interested that she nearly forgot that on the morrow Florence would have started on the journey to Boston.

The girls had climbed to the top of the wall, and were talking earnestly when suddenly Florence exclaimed: "Oh, dear! There comes grandfather to meet me. I must run. Goodbye, dear, dear Pen. I'll always keep your piece of money. Always! Always!" and before Penny could respond Florence had slipped from the wall and was running to meet her grandfather.

For a few moments Penelope sat quite still watching her; and when Florence turned and waved her hand Penny waved back. Then she too slid down from the wall, but she did not hurry toward home. Leaning against the warm rocks Penny began to cry. She would never see Florence again, she said to herself, never again. She put her hand to her neck and clasped the little gold locket with a sense of comfort. "I'm glad I gave her my piece of money," she whispered to herself.

CHAPTER X

A STRANGE ENCOUNTER

IT was an uneasy night for the Balfour household. Twice Mrs. Balfour was awakened by the sound of steps; and, peering from her window, was sure that she saw the figure of a man running across the field toward the highway. And later on, the kitchen clock had just struck twelve when the faint rumble of wheels came to her ears. Ted, thinking of the stolen sheep, lay long awake wondering how soon the cows would be driven away, and if even the hens and chickens would be left; while Penny crept out of bed as soon as she fancied her mother was asleep, and knelt at her open window to watch the distant lights of Stone House. She too had seen the shadowy figure creeping across the field, and whispered, "'Tis Black Aleck." And Penny noticed what her mother did not see—another figure moving about in the Balfour field. "It looks like a calf," thought Penny; and then decided that it might be a deer, as it was not uncommon for an occasional deer to be seen feeding in the open fields. Before midnight the last light at Stone House was extinguished; and Penny crept back to bed where she lay listening for the sound of the Dickinson coach when it should pass on the highway, and as soon as the rumble of wheels died away Penny's sleepy eyes closed.

Both Ted and Penny slept late the next morning, and it was Mrs. Balfour who opened the door to discover a big hamper on the steps. A letter addressed to her was fastened to the handle, and when Mrs. Balfour finished reading it she knew all that Florence had told Penny on the previous day. Ted listened in amazement when his mother read him the letter. It was a friendly note, asking Mrs. Balfour to accept the contents of the hamper as a neighborly gift, but it was the last page of the letter that made Ted open his eyes: "Florence wants Ted to have her pony, so Black Aleck has turned him into your lower field, and left the pony cart and harness near the stone wall."

Penelope came into the kitchen just as her mother finished reading the letter. The little gold chain was around her neck, and the locket showed brightly against her faded dress. "Oh! That was Florence's surprise!" she exclaimed, as she saw the hamper and heard about the pony.

"There is nothing but surprises in these troublous days," said Mrs. Balfour, drawing the hamper into the kitchen. "But the Dickinsons were indeed kind to send us these things." As she opened the hamper she gave a little exclamation of pleasure, and drew out a roll of blue sprigged muslin. "Look, Penny! This is to make you a Sunday dress."

As Penny took the pretty muslin in her hands she forgot that Florence had really gone, and her face beamed with delight, and she at once recalled the invitation to visit the minister's wife.

"Will you make it up right away, mother, so I can wear it when I go to see Mrs. Godfrey?"

"Indeed I will!" promised Mrs. Balfour; "and see this piece of scarlet cloth! 'Twill make you a fine cape come cold weather!"

"I wish 'twas blue," said Penny, recalling the scarlet coats of the British soldiers.

"And here is a roll of excellent cambric," continued Mrs. Balfour, "and some fine knitting yarn."

The lower part of the hamper was filled with packages of sugar, spices and wax candles; and Mrs. Balfour again exclaimed over the generous kindness of her Tory neighbors.

"Florence gave me this yesterday!" said Penny, holding up her locket, "and I am always going to keep it. Florence said they were going to England."

Ted ran down the field to look at the pony. The little creature had always been a pet, and when Ted called its name, "Top, Top," it came trotting toward him.

"Top" was snow white, and all the children of Warwick Village thought Florence Dickinson the most fortunate girl in the world to own such a pony. Ted led the pony toward the watering-trough for a drink, and then to the kitchen door for Penny and Mrs. Balfour to pet and admire.

"Too bad the squire had to go away," Ted thought, as he again let the pony loose to feed in the field, and started off to his work in the garden.

It was a busy morning for Mrs. Balfour, for Penelope pleaded that the blue muslin dress be cut and begun. "For the minister's wife may come very soon now," she urged; and the dainty material was cut in breadths for the skirt, and basted for Penny to stitch; and the little girl sat down on the door-step and worked happily all the morning. After dinner she was eager to begin again, but Mrs. Balfour shook her head and sent her to help Ted in the garden.

"And you will have to wear your best sunbonnet every day now, Penny. You are getting as brown as a nut."

Penny sighed as her mother said this, for since the adventure at Tiverton, when the man had taken her blue sunbonnet with the squire's letter hidden under the lining, Penny had run about the farm bareheaded.

"I say, Pen, wasn't Florence fine to give me the pony? I'll drive you to church next Sunday!" said Ted as they worked together culling the weeds from the garden.

"Truly! Will you truly, Ted?" responded Penny, in great delight; and then, before Ted could answer, she exclaimed, "I won't go! And I won't wear that blue muslin dress either!" and to Ted's surprise Penny stopped pulling the weeds, and began crying.

"Whatever is the matter, Pen?" he asked anxiously.

"We—we're acting just as if all we cared about was *things*," sobbed the little girl, "as if we were so glad to get the white pony and the muslin dress that we didn't care if Florence was gone."

"But we do care," Ted responded soberly; "and I guess Florence wants us to enjoy the pony or she would have given him to somebody else. But we won't drive him to church, Pen."

The girl wiped her eyes. "P'raps we'd better go to church in the pony-cart after all, Ted," she said, "if I wear my blue muslin," and Penelope could not help smiling at the thought of the beautiful dress on which her mother was now at work.

"All right," responded Ted pleasantly. "Say, Pen! I believe that's the minister's chaise coming over the road from the village."

"Yes, Ted!" responded Penny eagerly. "There's not another roan horse in the township save Mr. Godfrey's."

As the chaise came nearer the children could see that it was Mrs. Godfrey, and that she was alone; and in a few moments the roan horse had stopped at the Balfours' gate, and Mrs. Balfour was hurrying down the path to welcome their guest.

"Ted!" whispered Penny, as her brother said he must go and lead the horse to the stable, "Ted, we mustn't say a word about the Dickinsons going away. The squire doesn't want the village people to know."

"Of course we won't!" responded Ted sharply; "they're neighbors, and perhaps they can't help being Tories."

Penelope hurried to the house to wash her face and hands and make herself tidy before greeting her kind friend. She knew that her mother would say nothing about the Dickinsons going away in the night; and Penny was quite sure that Mrs. Godfrey had come to invite her for the promised visit, and this proved to be the case, for as Penelope crossed the yard to the seat under the oak tree, where Mrs. Balfour was entertaining her guest, she heard Mrs. Godfrey say: "How soon can you spare Penelope for the visit she has promised me?"

Then, as Penny came nearer, Mrs. Godfrey turned to smile and greet her, and said: "I hope you want to come very soon, my dear?"

"Oh, yes!" responded Penny, in so earnest a tone that Mrs. Godfrey must have been quite sure that the little girl was looking forward to a great pleasure.

Penny seated herself beside the minister's wife, and watched her with admiring eyes. "When I grow up I hope I will look just like Mrs. Godfrey, and talk just the way she does, and smile just the way she smiles," thought the little girl. "But I s'pose I can't!" and she sighed a little, remembering that her own eyes were blue, while Mrs. Godfrey's eyes were brown. "But I can smile the way she does," resolved Penny, and at once began "practicing"; until Mrs. Balfour, who had been watching her little daughter with anxious eyes, exclaimed:

"What is the matter, Penny, dear? Have you the toothache?"

"No, ma'am," responded Penny, in great surprise. "What made you think I had the toothache?"

"You were twisting your lips so queerly," answered Mrs. Balfour.

This was rather discouraging, but Penelope resolved to watch Mrs. Godfrey more closely, and to practice the smile before the little gilt-framed mirror in her own room. Penny had been so occupied with her own thoughts and her admiration of Mrs. Godfrey, that she had not paid much heed to the conversation; but she now heard a word that made her all attention.

"We hear the loyal people of Newport are nearly discouraged," Mrs. Godfrey was saying. "The British soldiers are like a swarm of locusts, stripping the shores of everything. It is time that the army at Tiverton made some effort to help the people."

"What could the army do?" Penny asked, and her question was rewarded by Mrs. Godfrey's charming smile as she answered:

"Oh, well, Colonel Will Barton likes a joke; he might capture a few British generals just for the fun of it."

And now Mrs. Godfrey declared that it was time for her to start for home, and Ted led the big roan horse to the gate and politely helped their visitor to her seat in the chaise.

"May not Penelope ride a little way with me?" she asked, and Mrs. Balfour cordially agreed; so Ted helped Penny to enter the chaise, and they drove away.

"I never rode in a chaise before," said Penny, as the big horse trotted along, the chaise swaying and swinging in a delightful manner.

"When you come to see me next week I will take you on a long drive," promised Mrs. Godfrey, "but I promised your mother to set you down at the ford to-day."

The ford was where the road crossed a shallow brook. There were stepping-stones, over which a person on foot could cross dry shod, but horses splashed through the shallow water, drawing cart or chaise after them. When they reached the stream Penny thanked Mrs. Godfrey for her ride, and promised to come on the following Thursday for the promised visit; then she stepped carefully down from the chaise, and stood watching it roll through the water and along the road until the overhanging trees hid it from view. Penny did not hurry on her way home; the sun was still high, and there was a pleasant shade under the big trees which bordered the road. Here and there she found wild strawberries, or the tender leaves of young checkerberries. There was a sleepy sound of bees hunting for sweets, and she was too near home to have any thought of fear. She was bareheaded, and now and then a ray of sunshine filtered through the leaves and danced about her yellow head. She had just gathered a spray of wild honeysuckle when a blue sunbonnet dropped directly in front of her.

"My sunbonnet!" she exclaimed. "The one the Tory took!"

"The very one, but I'm not a Tory," said a laughing voice, and looking up Penny saw the same tall man, in the same ragged clothes, who had taken the precious letter. For a moment Penny was afraid, and she looked about as if she wanted to run away. Then she heard the man say, "I am an American, and I have come away from Tiverton to bring back your sunbonnet and to find out where and how you got that letter and to whom you meant to give it."

As the man spoke he stepped back a little so that he was nearly hidden by the underbrush, but could look up and down the road and see the approach of any traveler.

"How did you find out where I lived?" asked Penny, fixing her wondering eyes on the man's face.

"Easy!" he responded laughingly. "Watched your brother's little boat, and thought the 'Freedom' must belong to a loyal American boy."

This made Penny gasp with surprise. No one else had ever guessed the real name of Ted's boat.

"Do you know my father?" she questioned.

"No; is he a soldier?" asked the man.

"Yes; he's at Tiverton," answered Penny. "We were going to see him when you stopped us.

"Was that it?" exclaimed the man. "Well, I made a mistake all around that day. Of course I thought you were Tory children carrying a message to some spy in our camp. You must forgive me, now I have brought back your sunbonnet."

"Was Colonel Barton glad to get the letter?" asked Penny.

"Yes, indeed; but he laughed well at me when he found out that it must have been brought by a friend. Well, since I have journeyed all the way from Colonel Barton's camp to bring back your sunbonnet, will you not forgive me and tell me your name?" And the tall man smiled at Penny, and the little girl smiled back as she responded:

"My name is Penelope Henrietta Balfour. I am named for both my grandmothers."

"A splendid idea," declared the man. "I've heard your brother's name is Sammy, and that he is a clever boy. Do you suppose he would do a service for Colonel Barton?"

"Oh, yes. But couldn't I do it?" answered Penny eagerly.

The man looked at her with friendly eyes, but shook his head. "I guess 'twould be wiser for Sammy

to undertake it," he said; "but you can help. Tell
Sammy to watch his boat every night and morning
from now on; and when he finds a small package
under the bow seat to carry it to Colonel Elliott as
fast as he can go. It may be Colonel Elliott will bring
Sammy back in his coach."

Penny's heart beat quickly. Here indeed was a great
adventure, for she had instantly resolved that she herself would carry this message. She would be "Sammy,"
and she would watch the boat.

"You understand, don't you?" questioned the tall
man. "Remember to tell Sammy that the very moment
he finds the package he is to be off to Old Warwick as
fast as he can go, telling his errand to no one, and give
the packet into Colonel Elliott's own hands."

"Yes, yes!" responded Penelope eagerly, and was
about to ask a question as to how "Sammy" could find
Colonel Elliott, when there was a rustle in the underbrush, and Penny's companion had disappeared. A
moment later she heard the sound of a horse's hoofs,
and a horseman came splashing through the ford. He
waved his hand to the little girl by the roadside, and
was out of sight before Penny had time even to wonder who he was.

For a little while Penelope waited, standing quite still,
hoping that the tall man would return. But at last she
realized that he had said all that he meant to say, and
that she would not see him again.

"I wish he hadn't brought back this sunbonnet," she thought, looking scornfully at that faded and abused article. "Of course I mustn't take it home. Ted would guess something in a minute." And Penny looked about for a place to hide it. This was easily found in the hollow end of an old log at the edge of the wood. "I must run every step of the way home," decided Penny, "or mother will think I have gone home with Mrs. Godfrey," and away she scampered at a great pace, her thoughts full of the remarkable happenings of the day, and of herself in Ted's outgrown clothes hurrying off with Colonel Barton's message.

CHAPTER XI

A DAY OF STORM

"MOTHER, who is Colonel Elliott?" Penny questioned as soon as she reached home, "and does he live in Old Warwick?"

"Colonel Elliott is one of our brave American soldiers. 'Tis hard to say where you'd find him these days. And so you are to go on your visit to the minister's wife next Thursday. It's a compliment indeed, Penny; and you must behave your best," and Mrs. Balfour smiled at Penny, thinking how excited the child was at the prospect of such a visit.

"Thursday!" exclaimed the little girl; "perhaps I can't go!" For she was thinking of the packet that she might find any day under the bow seat of the "Modeerf."

"Yes, indeed, you shall surely go," her mother responded; "the blue muslin shall be finished for you to wear, and Theodore will drive you over in the pony-cart."

Penny did not say any more, but went up-stairs and looked to see that the homespun trousers were where she had hidden them. She hunted up an old blouse of her brother's and put it with the trousers. Then she went and looked in the little gilt-framed mirror which hung near the window. But she did not practice smiling "like Mrs. Godfrey," as she had meant to do only that afternoon, but peered into the glass with firm-set lips and serious eyes. "If my hair was short I'd look 'most like Ted, only smaller," she thought. "I'll have to cut it off!" she resolved, grasping her yellow braid and looking at it accusingly. "The very minute I find the packet I'll cut it off." Then Penny sighed a little, remembering that her father had often said that no little girl in all the world had prettier hair than his Penelope, and thinking how sorry he would be to find her with hair just like Ted's.

"Perhaps he'll be proud to think I could help," she thought; and then she heard Ted calling her to come down to the garden and see how well the new peas were growing.

Ted wondered a little that Penny had so little to say, but decided that she must be thinking about Florence. Even the blue muslin dress could not make her forget all that the tall man had told her, or the promise she had given that the package should be delivered to Colonel Elliott. "Probably there will be writing on the package to tell me where to find him," Penny decided, as she thought the matter over. Then she remembered that the man had said that "Sammy" must start the moment the package was found; and at this thought Penny left the garden, without a word to Ted, and ran toward the house, resolved to carry "Sammy's" clothes to the shore and hide them so that she would not be delayed. "I must take my scissors, too, so I can cut this braid off," she thought. And now the little girl was on the alert for a chance to slip out of the house with her bundle without being seen. She stayed in her room peering out from the window at Ted, busy in the garden; and she could hear her mother busy in the room below. It was nearly supper-time, and in a few minutes Mrs. Balfour called and Penny slipped the bundle into the closet and went down to supper.

"The air feels like rain," Ted declared as they all sat down at the table, "and there are black clouds beyond the islands."

"Yes," responded Mrs. Balfour. "I think 'twill be a stormy night."

"Oh, dear!" exclaimed Penny dropping her spoon, and leaning back in her chair with such an expression of despair on her face that both Ted and his mother began to laugh.

"I don't think you ought to laugh. I don't want it to rain," said Penny.

This made Ted laugh more than ever. "Well, you ought to have said so before the moon changed. It's too late now," he said.

"What has the moon got to do with it?" asked Penny scornfully.

"Everything," declared Ted. "You ask anybody who lives near the shore and they'll tell you that there are wet moons and dry moons. And this is a wet moon. Shouldn't be surprised if it rained the rest of the month."

"Oh, dear!" said Penelope again, in such a hopeless tone that Mrs. Balfour, thinking that her little daughter feared a postponement of her visit to Mrs. Godfrey, said:

"It will probably be a fine, pleasant day on Thursday, Penny. Do not look so far ahead for trouble."

But Penelope's face did not brighten. And when, before they had finished supper, the rain began to fall steadily, she was a very sober-faced little girl.

"I suppose Pen's feeling bad about Florence," Ted whispered to his mother, as he took the milk pails and ran off toward the barn.

It rained hard all that night, and as Penny lay awake listening to the drops on the roof and the wind in the branches of the trees, she wondered if the tall stranger expected her to go to the shore rain or shine, and if she would have to go in search of Colonel Elliott in a pouring rain, with the wind sweeping clouds of mist across the bay.

"Perhaps he was thinking of storms when he said 'twas a boy's errand," she thought, and remembered how proud and eager Ted would be to carry such a message whatever the weather might be. "Perhaps I ought to tell Ted. Of course the man meant Ted when he said 'Sammy,'" she reflected, and then remembered that Ted had promised their mother not to go off on any secret journey. With this comforting thought the little girl, resolving that no storm should prevent her keeping her promise, went to sleep.

"Where's Ted?" Penny asked next morning as she came into the kitchen.

"He has run down to the shore to see that the boat is all right. There was a heavy surf all night," answered Mrs. Balfour.

The rain was still falling heavily, and a strong wind sweeping across the harbor.

"'Twill be a good day to work on the muslin dress," Mrs. Balfour said, as she saw Penny standing looking out the window. "You shall hem the flounce, while I finish the waist," she continued. "We will draw our chairs close to the window where we can see Ted when he comes from the shore." Mrs. Balfour's tone was very cheerful, and when Penny saw the muslin dress all ready for the flounce her face brightened. "There will be sufficient muslin for a sash!" declared Mrs. Balfour. And at this good news Penelope smiled happily, and put on her shining silver thimble and sat down beside her mother quite ready to forgive the "wet moon."

In a few moments they saw Ted running across the field from the shore.

"The 'Modeerf' is all right," he declared, as he opened the door. "I've pulled her up on the bank and turned her over; so now it can rain all it wants to," and closing the door Ted was off toward the barn.

In one corner of the barn Ted had put up a partition and called the enclosure his workshop. Here he spent many happy hours on stormy days working busily over bits of wood which he made into neat boxes, or making a footstool or table for his mother. But to-day he ran past the barn and across the pasture toward Bayberry Hill. Ted was barefooted and bareheaded; and his homespun blouse and trousers did not easily soak through, and when they did Ted was not at all troubled. He was used to being out in all kinds of weather, and knew that a good wetting did him no harm. As Ted came up from the shore he had seen a number of men on Bayberry Hill, and had instantly resolved to discover if possible who they were and what errand brought them to Balfour farm in such a storm.

Ted knew every rock and bush on the pasture slope, and when he reached the top of the hill he was careful to keep well sheltered from discovery by any watchful eye. From behind a ledge of gray rock he looked down the farther slope of the hill to the shore, and as he looked a sudden exclamation escaped him. "Tories!" exclaimed the boy, as he counted five big whale-boats drawn up on the shore, and hovering near them a number of men.

"They must have put in here last night," thought Ted. "After our cows, probably, and waiting for the wind to go down so they can get back to Prescott's camp."

Ted waited to see no more. He was resolved that they should not carry off his cows, and hurried back to the barn, where he decided to stay until he was sure that the "Tories," as he believed the men to be, had departed. "There are so many of them that perhaps they're on a regular raid," thought the boy, a little fearfully.

All day the wind blew and the rain came down steadily; and when at sunset the clouds lightened and the wind ceased Mrs. Balfour gave a sigh of relief. "I am surely glad that the storm is over," she said, "for you children have been as uneasy as stormy petrels. Now the sun is out, and I do hope Ted will hurry in to supper. And you, Penny! Why, wet as it is, a run out-of-doors before bedtime will do you good."

Penny was now her own smiling self again. She was quite sure that there could be no message in the boat for her to carry; nevertheless she resolved to get her bundle to the shore that very night.

Ted had made a second trip to the hill, and had seen that the boats were being put in readiness for departure. He was puzzled now, and began to believe that the men were not Tories after all, and wondered if they might not be Americans. "I won't tell mother about them until they have gone," he decided as he came in to supper.

Neither Ted nor his mother saw Penny when, with the bundle tightly clasped in her arms, she ran across the field toward the shore. She found the boat turned over as Ted had left it. "I'll look, but of course I won't find any package," thought the little girl, kneeling in the wet grass and reaching under the bow seat of the boat. But her hand touched something wrapped in a bit of oilcloth, and she drew it out.

There was a slip of paper fastened to the package, and in roughly printed letters Penny read:

> *"Deliver to Colonel Elliott. At House*
> *Next Assembly House."*

"I guess he didn't know that I could read writing," was Penny's first thought; and then she remembered that this was the message. It must be delivered as soon as she could find Colonel Elliott.

"I must go now. Just as soon as I can put on Ted's clothes, and cut off my hair," thought Penny, and began to unroll the bundle.

CHAPTER XII

"SAMMY"

"I'm glad I know just where to go," thought Penelope, as she reread the direction on the packet. Every child near Warwick knew and admired the Assembly House, built in 1726, with its unique porch and overhanging roof. It was three miles distant from the Balfour farm, and Penny and Ted had often walked there and back.

It was a queer little figure that crept along through the wet bushes toward the highway. Penny was barefooted and bareheaded; Ted's outgrown clothes, pulled hastily on over her own garments, were still too large for Penny. She had found it a difficult matter to cut off her thick braid of hair, and as she held its yellow length in her hand she had looked at it a little sorrowfully, and tucked it away in her blouse.

"I'm glad it isn't dark yet," she thought, looking cautiously around as she reached the road, "and I hope mother won't miss me. I can get back before morning."

The road was muddy, and the overhanging trees sent down little showers now and then; but the sky was clear and the setting sun had left its golden reflection along the distant horizon. At first Penny ran along the wet road, keeping as close to the trees as possible so that any chance traveler along the highway might not see her.

By the time she reached the ford the twilight had deepened into dusk, and Penny splashed through the stream without making any effort to find the stepping-stones. She went sturdily along up the hill, and soon came out on the open stretch of road facing the harbor. "I'm half-way there now," she thought, stopping to rest for a moment and looking across the water toward the distant islands.

As Penny looked she saw what seemed to her like a number of dark shadows over the water, moving down the bay toward Prudence Island. Then, as her eyes became more accustomed to the movement of the waves, she suddenly realized that the shadows were boats. But Penny did not think much about it, for it was no uncommon sight to see boats moving along the shores, or from island to island.

"I wonder if I can ever tell mother and father about this?" thought the little girl, clasping the package more closely and hurrying along. The road soon left the shore, and for the rest of the distance to the cross-roads the way led through the shadows of a thick wood; and now Penny began to run again. The soft pad of her bare feet made no more noise than did those of a rabbit which scuttled across her path and disappeared in the shadows.

It was a very muddy and tired little figure that crept up the path of the house nearest the Assembly House and stood hesitating on the porch steps. She could see a glimmer of candlelight in one of the front rooms, and, after a moment's hesitation, Penny went bravely up the steps, lifted the knocker and jumped back as it clanged down.

The door opened so quickly that the child was sure that some one must have been standing there waiting for the summons.

"Does—does Colonel Elliott live here?" faltered Penny, as the light from the open door showed her the tall figure of an elderly woman, who looked sharply at the queer little figure on her threshold.

"'Tis plain that you are no child of Warwick Village to ask such a question. This is the Arnold house; but a message is expected here for Colonel Elliott, and will reach him safely," and the woman reached out her hand and Penny slipped the little package into it. The door closed as suddenly as it had opened. The glimmer of candle-light disappeared. Everything seemed very still to the little girl standing alone on the porch steps in the darkness of the summer night.

"Oh, dear!" she exclaimed. "The man said perhaps Colonel Elliott would give me a ride home in his coach, and he isn't here!" and Penny suddenly realized that she was a very tired little girl, that home was a long distance away, and that the night had grown very dark.

She went slowly down the path and turned her face toward the homeward road. Suddenly she heard the sound of a horse's hoofs, and looked back just in time to see the dark outline of a man on horseback dash out from the stableyard of the Arnold house and speed off toward the Providence road.

"Oh, dear!" said Penny again, and her exclamation had a very discouraged tone.

It was midnight when Penny reached Balfour farm; and now, for the first time, she began to wonder how she could reach her room without awakening her mother or Ted. Usually the front and back doors were both secured on the inside by stout wooden bars. If they were so fastened to-night Penny knew that it would be an easy matter to push up one of the kitchen windows and climb in. She tried the back door, and at her gentle push it swung smoothly open, and Penny found herself in the dark kitchen. She crept softly to the narrow hallway, and made her way up the curving stairway and into her own room, and stood there a breathless but triumphant Penelope. She had carried the message, and returned through the darkness safely to her own room. But to Penny the greatest part of her triumph was that she had not wakened either her mother or Ted.

And now she quietly slipped out of her clothing, and, without a thought of her muddy feet or shorn head, crept in between the clean sheets and was soon asleep;

nor did the disturbance which aroused Mrs. Balfour and Ted in the early morning waken the tired little girl.

"Ted," Mrs. Balfour called, when awakened by the sound of voices at no great distance from the house, "I fear 'tis a party of Tories who have landed at the cove."

It did not take Ted long to dress, and in a few moments he and his mother were standing in the doorway looking in amazement at a group of men gathered under the big oak.

"Those are American soldiers, Ted! And they have a prisoner!" she declared.

As she spoke a tall man left the group and hastened toward the house.

"I trust we have not frightened or disturbed your household, madam?" he said as he came near. "I am Colonel Barton, at your service; and the gentleman yonder, in the cloak, is my prisoner, General Prescott. My men were detained by the storm, or he would be in Providence ere this."

In answer to Mrs. Balfour's eager questions he told of the night's great adventure. The American boats had slipped down the harbor, and midway between Newport and Bristol Ferry had made a landing and concealed their boats, and then gone directly to the farmhouse where General Prescott made his headquarters.

"'Twas an easy matter, I assure you, madam!" said the colonel. "We had but to overpower the sentries, break open the general's door and force him to come with us. 'Tis not more than eight hours since my men sailed from this very shore. There has not been a slip; that is, if our message was carried to Warwick Village?" and he looked questioningly toward Ted. But a sudden commotion among his men made him hurry toward them.

"What did he mean by a message, Ted? And why did he look at you so closely?" asked Mrs. Balfour. "But this is indeed great news. 'Twill be a day famous in history," she continued, without waiting for an answer to her question.

There came the sound of the rumbling of a coach, and a moment later a big coach, driven by an officer of the American army, stopped at the Balfour gate. Securely guarded, the British general was thrust into the coach; the men filed back to their boats and pulled away toward their camp in Tiverton, and the coach drove off toward Warwick.

Colonel Barton ran back to the door. "You have a brave and trustworthy son, madam," he said, "and," turning toward Ted, "you, Sammy, will hear from us again;" and he was gone, leaving Ted and his mother standing puzzled and amazed; and again Mrs. Balfour repeated her question:

"What did he mean by a message, Ted?"

"I don't know," responded the boy, "nor why he should call me 'Sammy.' I wish I had known those were Americans when I saw them on the shore."

THE BRITISH GENERAL WAS THRUST INTO THE COACH

To himself Ted added that had he known he would have, by some means, been one of that triumphant company who had sailed past British ships and taken a great general captive.

"'Tis too bad Pen could not have seen Colonel Barton and the coach," said Ted, as he and his mother turned back to the house.

"I wonder she did not wake," said Mrs. Balfour; "but the sleep will do her no harm, though she crept off to bed last night without my knowing it. Ted, this is a happy day for us. With such good news 'tis more than likely that your father can get a furlough and come home, for a time at least."

"Mother," said Ted, "are you sure Pen is in bed?"

"Of course she is! Where would she be?" answered Mrs. Balfour.

"May I go and make sure?" asked the boy.

"Why, Ted, what are you thinking of?" but Ted was tiptoeing up the stairs, and, in a moment, peering in at Penny who was still sleeping soundly.

"Yes, she's there all right," Ted said as he came back to the kitchen, "and sleeping as sound as a door-mouse."

"Whatever made you think that the child was not in her room, Ted?" questioned his mother.

"Well, I guess it was what Colonel Barton said about a message," answered the boy. "It sounded as if he thought some one in this house had been given a message to carry. And you know Pen is always planning to do some great thing to help the Americans, and I thought she'd got the chance."

"That would be a boy's errand," responded Mrs. Balfour, "but we will have a fine tale to tell Penny when she does wake up," and Mrs. Balfour went about her usual duties with a lighter heart than she had known for many a day. This capture of Prescott meant happier days for loyal Americans, she was sure of that; and as she worked she sang:

> "Ruin seize thee, ruthless king!
> Confusion on thy banners wait;
> Tho' fanned by Conquest's crimson wing,
> They mock the air with idle state."

And Penny was aroused from her slumbers by her mother's triumphant song. For a moment she lay half awake, wondering sleepily what made her feel so tired. Then she remembered all that had happened the night before, and put her hand on her shorn head thinking how light and queer it felt. "I s'pose I must get up," she said aloud, and then she found herself facing a great difficulty! What reason could she give her mother and Ted for cutting off her hair? "I won't give any reason," resolved Penny. "I'll just say that I wanted to cut it off," and with this decision Penny slipped out of bed. "Gracious!" she exclaimed, looking down at her feet, still stained with the mud, "and I went to bed with those feet."

CHAPTER XIII

THE DAY AFTER

PENNY went slowly down the stairs and opened the kitchen door. The clock had struck nine, and the little girl could not remember that she had ever before slept so late. Mrs. Balfour was just coming from the pantry, and looked smilingly toward her little daughter. But the smile vanished as she noticed the shorn head, and she lifted both hands in surprise as she exclaimed: "Penelope Henrietta Balfour! What has happened to your hair?"

Penny put a protecting hand over a particularly rebellious lock that persisted in falling over her forehead, and replied faintly: "I cut it off."

"Of all things! And you invited to visit the minister's wife to-morrow! I never saw the beat of it. I have a good mind to send you straight back to bed," and Mrs. Balfour looked at Penny very sternly.

"I'd just as soon go back to bed," responded Penny in so meek a tone that her mother instantly relented, and said in her usual kindly voice:

"I've kept your porridge hot. Get your bowl and a pitcher of milk and eat your breakfast."

Penelope obeyed eagerly for she was very hungry. As she ate her mother came and stood beside her and touched her cropped head.

"I can't understand your doing such a thing, dear child. You know your father was always so proud of your thick braid. What will he say?"

Penny choked a little as her mother said this. She began to feel very unhappy, and almost to wish that she had left the package under the seat of the boat. She was still sleepy and tired, and it seemed very hard to be blamed when she had been trying to help the Americans.

"As soon as you finish your breakfast, Penny, I will trim your hair more evenly, and perhaps I can crochet you a net of that ball of yellow silk to cover your poor little bare head," said Mrs. Balfour, noticing that her little daughter looked pale and tired, and wondering if this sudden freak of cutting off her hair might not mean that Penny was going to be ill.

So Penny was seated in a chair by the window, and her mother trimming her uneven locks when Ted came in. "Don't tell him!" Penelope whispered, and when Ted exclaimed: "I say, mother! What are you cutting off Pen's hair for?" Mrs. Balfour made no response. "I suppose Pen's teased you into it," he concluded.

"I haven't told Penny about what happened this morning," said Mrs. Balfour.

"It was great, Pen! Just think, Colonel Barton was right at our front door. And a coach with Colonel

Elliott came driving up and took the prisoner off to Providence," said Ted, after Mrs. Balfour had told the story of Prescott's capture.

"The strangest part of it all," said Mrs. Balfour, "is that Colonel Barton seemed to think that Ted had done him some service; carried a message or something of the sort, and called him 'Sammy,' and said that 'Sammy' would hear from him again. Why, Pen!" For Penny, who had sat still and nearly breathless while the wonderful story was being told, now burst into a storm of sobs and tears. "I do believe the child is ill," said Mrs. Balfour, as she tried to comfort Penny.

"Don't cry, 'Smiling Sally,'" urged Ted. "Mother thinks perhaps father will soon be coming home." But this only made Penny cry all the harder, and Ted took himself off, thinking it was too bad that Penny had not wakened in time to see Colonel Barton.

Mrs. Balfour made Penny lie down on the comfortable sofa in the sitting-room.

"You must have caught a little cold last night," she said, as she put a pillow for Penny's head.

"Last night!" echoed Penny, half afraid that her mother had guessed the great secret.

"Why, yes, dear, when you went running down to the shore. You went off to bed so quietly I did not know when you went," responded Mrs. Balfour. "Now take a little nap, for sleep is the best medicine," and Mrs. Balfour went back to her work, leaving her daughter alone.

For a little while Penny lay quite still thinking over all that her mother and Ted had told her. Her heart beat quickly at the thought of the great general traveling off to Providence in the coach she had summoned.

"But nobody knows I took the message. Everybody will always think it was Ted; and I walked all night and cut off my hair," thought Penny. But then came a new thought: "Anyway, I helped. It's no matter whether anybody knows or not," and comforted by this assurance Penny went fast asleep, but was wide awake and quite ready for the noonday meal.

"You look like a little Dutch girl, Penny, now that your hair is cut short," said her mother; "but with a net of yellow silk and a new blue muslin dress, you will look fine indeed."

In the afternoon Penelope and her mother took their work out under the big oak. Mrs. Balfour crocheted the soft silk net, and Penny sewed the dainty little frills of white muslin into the neck and sleeves of her new dress. The sunlight flickered between the green leaves as if searching for the golden silk and for the girl's yellow hair.

Mrs. Balfour had been telling Penny again all that Colonel Barton had said; before she finished Ted came across the field and stood leaning against his mother's chair.

"I'll show Pen just how he walked and bowed," declared Ted, running back a few paces, and then coming toward them in a manner very like that of Colonel Barton, and sweeping his old hat from his head Ted bowed before his mother and said, "I hope you have not been disturbed, madam," and then, as nearly as he could remember it, repeated the morning's conversation. Penny watched him with eager eyes. "As for you, Sammy," concluded Ted, turning toward Penny, and resting his hand upon her shoulder, "you are a brave boy! And you shall hear from us later on."

"Oh!" gasped the little girl, who was now almost sure that Ted had discovered her secret.

"Don't look so frightened, Pen," laughed Ted. "Colonel Barton won't hurt me. Perhaps he found out about that letter we tried to get to him in Tiverton."

But this remark, so near to what Penny knew to be the truth, only made her gasp again, and Ted looked at her in surprise, and exclaimed: "Well, Pen, I don't see what ails you. Ever since Florence went away you haven't seemed to enjoy anything."

"It's all been so queer," responded Penny.

"Indeed it has," agreed her mother, "'but now we have pleasant things before us. You are going on a visit to-morrow, and perhaps your father will come any day."

"And perhaps Florence will come back!" suggested Ted.

With all these pleasant things to think of Penny was soon her smiling self once more, and when they walked toward the house she thought to herself that she would not change places with any little girl on the shores of Narragansett Bay. "I don't believe any other girl ever carried a message to Colonel Elliott," she thought happily, and then looked admiringly at her pretty new dress which she was carrying very carefully, and at the golden net. "The net is prettier than hair," she declared, as her mother slipped it over her head.

CHAPTER XIV

POMP AND PRIDE

"I wish Florence could see how pretty my muslin dress is," said Penny, as her mother tied her broad sash and said:

"There, now you are all ready except putting on your sunbonnet, and you look very nice indeed."

Penny wore her white open-work knit cotton stockings, and low shoes with straps over the instep. The slender gold chain and locket was around her neck and the silken net over her short hair gave the little girl an unusually prim and sedate appearance.

As Penny looked at her reflection in the mirror she decided that she liked the net. "It makes me look almost grown up, doesn't it, mother?" she asked, and her mother's reply: "It certainly does make you look older," made the little girl smile happily.

"I wish I didn't have to wear a sunbonnet, and cover my net all up," said Penny when her mother brought the white sunbonnet for her to put on.

"'Tis much more suitable for you to wear the sunbonnet," responded her mother, "and here comes Ted."

There was a rattle of wheels and a loud "Whoa," and there was Ted at the gate with the white pony and the low cart swung between two big wheels.

"Isn't the pony white!" exclaimed Penny.

"Ought to be. I scrubbed him well this morning, and brushed and combed him, too," answered Ted, as he helped her to her seat in the cart.

Mrs. Balfour gave them her last charges and kissed them good-bye, and stood at the gate watching the cart until a turn in the road hid it from view; then she turned back to the house with a smiling face, and her heart full of happy thoughts. She was quite sure that there were not better children in all the world than her own boy and girl, and she sent a grateful thought to the Dickinsons for the gifts which had brought so much pleasure to Ted and Penny.

The pony trotted briskly over the smooth road, picked his way carefully across the ford, and seemed to enjoy the journey as much as his passengers.

"That's the Arnold house," announced Penny, as they reached the crossroads, passed the Assembly House, and turned into the road leading to the minister's house.

"How do you know?" asked Ted, in a surprised tone, and Penny felt a sudden dismay at having spoken.

"Well, isn't it?" she responded.

"Perhaps it is. I heard Colonel Elliott say that breakfast would be ready for General Prescott at the Arnolds'," answered Ted. "Don't you think 'twas funny, Pen," he continued, "that Colonel Barton should call me 'Sammy'?"

"Y-es," faltered the little girl, and then exclaimed, "Look, Ted! There is Mrs. Godfrey at her gate, looking for us," and she waved her hand.

In a moment Ted had brought the pony to a standstill directly in front of where Mrs. Godfrey was standing, and, hat in hand, was making his most polite bow.

"And what a fine Penelope it is," exclaimed Mrs. Godfrey, as Penny jumped from the cart. "Tell your mother we will bring her safely home before twilight," she said to Ted, taking Penelope by the hand as Ted turned the pony's head toward home and drove off.

Penny had never seen the minister's house before, and looked admiringly at the pretty garden through which a neat gravel path led to the front door. On each side of the path was a row of crimson peonies, nodding their heavy heads of bloom as if to welcome the little visitor. Beyond the peonies were beds of sweet-william; and beyond those other flowers whose names Penelope did not know, and the air was full of their fragrance.

"Mr. Godfrey is away for the day," said the minister's wife, as she led Penny up the path, "so you and I will be quite by ourselves."

Penny was delighted to hear this, and was now quite sure that she was going to have a wonderful time. Mrs. Godfrey untied the strings of the sunbonnet and as she took it off she looked at Penny in amazement.

"Oh, child!" she exclaimed.

Penny had quite forgotten her cropped head, but now she quickly remembered it, and her face flushed uncomfortably. She wished that she could tell Mrs. Godfrey all about it, and about the tall man who had brought back her sunbonnet.

"But what a pretty net," continued Mrs. Godfrey.

"Oh!" Penny suddenly exclaimed, for coming across the square hall were two small, white woolly dogs. They came up and stopped directly in front of Penny, looking first at her and then at their mistress, and making friendly little barks.

"They expect to be introduced," said Mrs. Godfrey laughingly. "This one with the blue ribbon is Pomp, and this is Pride." As she spoke their names, "Pomp" and "Pride," each stood up on his hind legs, bobbed his head and gave a sharp bark.

"They knew just what you said," exclaimed Penny delightedly.

"Of course they knew," responded Mrs. Godfrey.

The little dogs now came very close to Penny, eager to make friends. She sat down on the lower step of the stairs and in a moment both the dogs were beside her.

"They are company for me," said Mrs. Godfrey. "My sister brought them when she came to visit me in the spring. I will let them entertain you a few minutes, Penny dear, while I step to the kitchen."

Penny was quite happy to have Pomp and Pride for companions, and when Mrs. Godfrey returned she found the little girl laughing with delight while the two woolly dogs frisked about her.

"Now you must come and see my garden," said Mrs. Godfrey, and then repeated the word "garden" several times, pointing a warning finger at Pomp and Pride.

The two little dogs instantly became very quiet, and when Penny and Mrs. Godfrey walked down the steps Pomp and Pride followed in a very dignified manner. They no longer frisked about Penny, nor made wild rushes at each other; neither did they roll themselves up until they looked like round woolly balls.

"It took me a long time," explained Mrs. Godfrey, noticing the puzzled look on Penny's face, "to make them understand what I meant when I said 'garden'; but they know now that they cannot race or run or roll about in my flower-beds."

There was a high brick wall on one side of Mrs. Godfrey's garden, and growing close against it were a number of plum trees whose branches had been trained to grow flat against the wall. In this pleasant corner of the garden stood a rustic summer-house. Dilly, the colored maid, was just spreading a white cloth over the round table. "I thought we should enjoy having our dinner out here," said Mrs. Godfrey.

"Yes, indeed!" agreed Penny enthusiastically, and watched Dilly with delighted eyes as she spread the table.

The dishes were covered with little pink roses, and at the place set for Penny was a luster mug, the inside

of which glowed with a wonderful pink. Dilly returned
from the kitchen with a tray, and now Penny realized
that she was hungry and looked approvingly on the
platter of cold sliced chicken, the dish of new peas, the
plate of round biscuit, and the dish of yellow custard
which Dilly set on the table.

Everything tasted as good as it looked, and Pomp
and Pride were rewarded for their good behavior
with choice bits of chicken. Penny was just finishing
her custard when Dilly appeared at the door of the
summer-house.

"The minister has sent the Perkins boy with a message," she announced, and stepped back. "You jes'
speak your message now," she said to the small boy
standing behind her, giving him a gentle shove
toward Mrs. Godfrey.

"The minister says he can't come home until late, and
that he hopes you'll keep the little girl for company,"
faltered the Perkins boy, who was thanked for bringing the message, and persuaded to sit down beside Mrs.
Godfrey and make a good luncheon.

"I'll let Dilly drive over and tell your mother
that I want you to stay with me until tomorrow,"
said Mrs. Godfrey, with her pretty smile as she
turned to Penny.

"I'll go," offered the Perkins boy. "My horse isn't a
mite tired," and so it was settled that he should take the

message to Mrs. Balfour, and that Penelope should remain as Mrs. Godfrey's guest until the next afternoon.

They were just leaving the summer-house when the click of the gate made them look in that direction. "There is Mrs. Arnold!" exclaimed Mrs. Godfrey, hastening forward to meet her guest.

Penny looked at the visitor, and stopped short. It was the woman to whom she had handed the package for Colonel Elliott.

"She will know me, I know she will! What shall I do?" thought Penny, turning as if to run away; but it was too late. She heard Mrs. Godfrey welcome her neighbor, and say:

"This is my little visitor, Penelope Balfour."

Penny made a curtsey, but did not dare raise her eyes. She heard the visitor say, "How do you do, Penelope?" and followed the two ladies to the house. Mrs. Arnold was telling the minister's wife of "Will Barton's" capturing the English general.

"A boy brought a message to my house that night," said Mrs. Arnold, after they were seated in the parlor, "a boy no larger than Penelope," and she turned a keen glance on the little girl, who was perched uneasily on the edge of the sofa. "Perhaps 'twas your brother?" she added.

"Oh, no, ma'am! My brother is a—a good deal larger than I am," replied Penny.

"I dare say. I only got a glimpse of the boy. But he was a brave lad, whoever he may be, and did the Colonies a good service," said the woman. "I guess you wish it had been your brother, now don't you?" she concluded, with a friendly nod toward the little girl.

"No'm—yes'm," answered Penny, not knowing quite what answer she was making, but feeling very pleased and happy, and wishing more than ever that she could tell the story of the message.

"But I s'pose I mustn't until the tall man says I may," she thought to herself, growing a little uncomfortable under the sharp looks which Mrs. Arnold now and then sent in her direction. But at last the visitor departed. Pomp and Pride escorted her as far as the door, and stood there in their most dignified manner until the gate clicked behind her; then they returned and curled themselves into round woolly balls at Penny's feet.

CHAPTER XV

SYLVIA

"OH, my!" exclaimed Penny, stopping short at the door of the sitting-room.

"What is it, my dear?" questioned Mrs. Godfrey, who was close behind her. They were just coming in from the dining-room where they had had supper, and Penny's sudden exclamation made Mrs. Godfrey stop and look at her little guest questioningly.

"It's that! It's those!" explained Penny, pointing toward the rug in front of the open fireplace. When Penny and Mrs. Godfrey left the sitting-room a half hour earlier Pomp and Pride, two woolly white balls, were lying on that rug. Now Penny looked, and could hardly believe her own eyes, for there were two small coal-black shiny creatures on the rug, and no trace of Pomp or Pride. Instantly Penny recalled the stories of "witch-work" that Black Hitty had told the little girls, and wondered to herself if some witch had come down the chimney and changed the little white dogs into the little black kittens lying on the hearth-rug.

"Oh, it's 'Flight' and 'Folly,'" laughed Mrs. Godfrey. "Just think of your being here all day and not seeing my black kittens. They will make friends without an introduction."

"I thought perhaps it was 'witch-work,'" said Penny, when she was comfortably seated on a low stool with Flight and Folly in her lap.

Mrs. Godfrey laughed again. Penny wondered if anybody else in all the world was as ready to laugh as the minister's wife.

"What do you know about witches?" asked the minister's wife.

"Black Hitty used to tell Florence and me witch stories," said Penny, smoothing Folly's black coat. "She says that there's a witch in every black crow that flies over a corn-field."

This made Mrs. Godfrey laugh so heartily that Penny found herself laughing, and ever after that the name "witch" always seemed very funny to her. While they were laughing steps sounded in the hallway and the minister entered the room. Penny was surprised to hear Mrs. Godfrey exclaim "Frederic!" as she ran forward to meet him. Penny wondered to herself if it could be right, even for Mrs. Godfrey, to call the minister "Frederic."

Penny stood up holding Flight under one arm and Folly under the other, and made her very best curtsey. The minister patted the golden net. "How do you like the names I gave the black kittens?" he asked.

This seemed more amazing to Penny than did the kittens themselves, but she answered that she thought the kittens' names sounded just like kittens.

"There, Grace! Did I not say exactly those words?" laughed the minister, and now Penny ventured to smile at him, and it was not long before she was sure that she should like the minister just as well as she did Mrs. Godfrey.

"All the town is wondering about the boy who left the message at the Arnold house," the minister said, as he spoke of Prescott's being under guard in Providence. "Colonel Barton thought it was your brother, Penny, but Theodore declares he knows nothing of it."

"No, it was not Ted," responded Penny, in so low a tone that Mrs. Godfrey thought the little girl must be sleepy, and hurried her off to bed.

When Penny entered the little room where she was to sleep she exclaimed again, for she was sure that there was not another room so pretty this side of Boston. The wall was hung with the most wonderful paper that Penny had ever seen. There were tall green trees, and blossoming roses, and birds; and walking among the roses were ladies, and small boys and girls. Before Penny could even think of saying her prayers she had to walk all about the room looking at this wonderful paper.

"Frederic sent to his brother in London for this paper," explained Mrs. Godfrey. "So you see it came across the Atlantic Ocean on purpose for this room."

The floor was covered with a bright carpet, and there was a bed with curtains of flowered chintz; the chairs were covered with chintz like the bed-curtains, and it was a very bright and cheerful room. But Penny was all ready for bed before she discovered another wonder.

"Oh!" she said, as her eyes rested on a little rocking-chair standing near the head of the bed, and holding a wonderful wax doll dressed in blue satin.

"That's my very own doll," explained Mrs. Godfrey. "She came from London, too, when I was just ten years old and lived in Newport. And she was such a fine doll that I was never allowed to play with her, and so I never cared very much about her. Her name is Sylvia. Now, good-night, dear child!" and Mrs. Godfrey went out and left Penny to go to sleep in the wonderful room.

Penny lay close to the edge of the curtained bed where she could see the faint outline of Sylvia in the little chair.

"I guess I should think Sylvia was a 'witch-doll' if I b'lieved in witches," she thought. "She is most too beautiful to be a truly doll." Then Penny thought over the long happy day with Pomp and Pride and Flight and Folly, but her last waking thought was the wish that she could again see the tall American soldier and that he would say she might tell who "Sammy" was, and then, for the first time, she remembered that the man himself believed that a boy named Sammy had carried the message for Colonel Elliott.

"Oh, dear!" she whispered to herself. "I do wish Florence was back at Stone House. I would tell Florence."

When Penny awoke the next morning she said aloud: "I haven't really waked up!" for just inside her doorway stood two little white dogs and two little black kittens. They did not make the slightest noise, but when Penny, suddenly remembering that she was visiting the minister's wife, sat up in bed the dogs and kittens scuttled out of the room. "Just as if they had only looked in to see if I were really here," thought the little girl; nor did she see them again until she went down-stairs quite ready for breakfast.

"What are you thinking about, Penny?" asked Mrs. Godfrey when she was tying the strings of Penny's sunbonnet just before they started for the drive to Balfour farm.

Penelope sighed. "I guess I daren't tell you," she responded slowly, "but I know I ought to. I was thinking that I was glad I said that verse in Sunday-school, because if I had not said it you would not have made friends with me, and I never should have seen Pomp and Pride or Flight and Folly, or Sylvia!" and now Penny began to cry, for she felt quite sure that after such a confession Mrs. Godfrey could never like her again.

There was indeed a puzzled look on Mrs. Godfrey's kind face as she put her arm about the little girl, but she said quickly: "We will always be friends, dear child. And as I told you, there was no harm in the verse you repeated. But you do not know who is going to drive to Balfour farm with us," and she led the way to the gate.

Penny dried her eyes and followed slowly. She had already said her good-byes to the minister, to Dilly, to the kittens and to Pomp and Pride; but she thought to herself that she supposed it must be the minister who would drive with them. But as she reached the side of the chaise, she saw a glimmer of blue satin.

"Sylvia!" she exclaimed in delight. For there in the chaise stood the little chair, and in it sat the wonderful Sylvia. "I am so glad. I was wishing my mother could see her," said the delighted little girl, "and she will be company for you on your way home."

What a wonderful ride that was for Penny! Mrs. Godfrey was quite sure that Sylvia would like to sit in Penelope's lap, and Penny quite forgot that she was too big to enjoy a doll's society. As they rode along Mrs. Godfrey told Penny the story of Sylvia's journey from London to New York and from New York to Newport, and before the story was quite finished they had reached Balfour farm.

Penelope was a very proud and happy little girl when she heard Mrs. Godfrey tell her mother that she, Penelope, had made the minister and his wife both wish that they had a little daughter exactly like Penelope Balfour. Then Sylvia and her chair were lifted from the chaise, and now Penny began to think that wonderful things would really never stop happening, for Mrs. Godfrey was saying: "And now Sylvia is yours, Penny. I have always thought her too fine a doll to take comfort with, but you seem to have made friends with her, and I think you will both be happy," and Penny found herself standing with the beautiful Sylvia in her arms, and the little chair on the grass beside her.

THERE IN THE CHAISE STOOD THE LITTLE CHAIR

Penny could never remember what she said to express her thanks to Mrs. Godfrey, or if she really thanked her at all. But in a moment she realized that Mrs. Godfrey was gone, and that Sylvia was her very own. Then how fast Penny talked, as she and her mother walked toward the house! How much there was to tell! The white puppies, the black kittens, the wonderful little room where she had slept, and Mrs. Arnold's visit.

"And what was the very best part of it all, dear child?" questioned Mrs. Balfour.

"The very best part of it all is coming home and telling you all about it," declared Penny happily. "But, mother, I do think that Mrs. Godfrey is wonderful. Do you know she never said a word about my hair's being cut off; she never asked a single question about it," Penney said, when she had changed her pretty muslin dress for her every-day gown, and put on the moccasin slippers instead of the kid ties she had worn on her visit. "She did not even look as if she wished she knew why I cut it off," continued the little girl.

"Well, Penny, Mrs. Godfrey is a lady, and ladies do not ask questions of visitors. But mothers ask questions; can't you tell me why you wanted your hair short?" responded her mother.

But Penny did not answer, and Mrs. Balfour decided that the little girl hardly knew what had prompted her to do such a thing.

CHAPTER XVI

NEIGHBORS OR TORIES?

TED and Penny were sure that their father would soon appear at Balfour farm, and every day Penny went to the top of Bayberry Hill and looked across the bay hoping for the sight of a boat that might bring him. Ted sailed the "Modeerf" out toward the islands, keeping a sharp outlook, but a week had passed by since Penny's visit to Mrs. Godfrey, and no news came from the Tiverton camp.

So many things had happened immediately after Squire Dickinson's departure that Penny at first did not really miss Florence. But now the days seemed very long, and she would often go and sit on the wall where she and Florence had so often lingered, and wish that her little playmate was again in the Stone House. Sylvia was a great comfort to Penny. She took the doll with her on many of her walks, and explained to Sylvia many things of which she could not speak to any one. The blue satin dress had been carefully put away, and Penny had made the doll a serviceable dress of pieces of brown checked gingham from her mother's "piece bag."

"Do you suppose father is ever coming, Ted?" she asked one morning as the brother and sister made their way to the shore. Penny had left Sylvia at home. Ted was carrying a small wooden pail and a number of tools.

"Of course he's coming," responded the boy. "We may see him any time. Everybody says that Colonel Barton's men dare do anything, and that now the English general is a prisoner the Americans are sure to win. Then father will be home to stay."

"Goody!" exclaimed Penny, who always felt as if she were being praised when Prescott's capture was spoken of. "What are you going to do with that yellow paint, Ted?" For as they reached the shore she had peeked into the bucket and discovered the yellow paint.

"Wait and see," responded Ted, selecting a brush from the package of tools he had been carrying.

Penny sat down close by the boat and watched him. After testing his brush to be quite sure that it was in good working order, Ted dipped it into the yellow paint, which he had carefully mixed, of oil and yellow ochre, and drew a broad splash over the name "Modeerf."

"Oh, Ted!" exclaimed Penny.

"You just wait!" said Ted. "I'm not going to sail a boat under a twisted name. I'm going to paint 'Freedom' in big letters on both sides, and we'll see if anybody dares to touch a boat with that name."

Penny looked at her brother admiringly. For a moment she almost decided to tell him that she had carried the mysterious message, but Ted had begun to speak again:

"I say, Pen, I'll bet anything that Squire Dickinson will come back."

"No, they won't ever come back," answered Penny, despondently.

Ted dipped his brush and drew a broad yellow splash over "Modeerf." Then he said: "What would you say if I told you that Hitty and Black Aleck are there now?"

Penny could hardly speak for a moment. Then she managed to say, "Wh-what makes you think that, Ted?"

"Saw 'em!" responded Ted; then glancing at his sister's astonished face he began to laugh.

"You look so funny, Pen," he exclaimed. "Your hair is half out of your net and hanging over your face, and you look as if you'd seen a witch!"

"There isn't any such thing as a witch, and never mind about my hair. Tell me about seeing Black Aleck and Hitty," said Penny.

"Tell me what made mother cut off your hair?" demanded Ted.

"She didn't," Pen answered before she thought, but Ted only laughed.

"I happened to see her with the scissors in her hand. But she didn't make a very good job of it," he responded. "Well, I saw smoke coming from Stone House chimney this morning, and I just ran over to see what was going on, and there was Hitty frying a chicken and Black Aleck half asleep on the porch."

"Well, that doesn't mean that the Dickinsons are coming back," said his sister; "it means that they will never come back; that they have gone to England. Did you speak to them?"

"No," said Ted. "I don't know why I didn't, but I just turned and ran. I didn't even tell mother."

Penny jumped up.

"I'm going right up there this minute," she declared, and before Ted could say a word she was running across the field toward Stone House, and in a short time was standing at the kitchen door.

"Land's sake, chile!" exclaimed Hitty. "Wha' you been a-doin' to you'self?"

"Never mind me, Hitty! Where's Florence?" demanded Penny.

"I nebber seen anybody look like you do! Your hair all witch-way," persisted Hitty. "I guess Missy Florence won't scursely know you."

"Where is she?" asked Penny.

"Well, jus' this perticular minute she's upstairs fas' asleep," said Hitty. "You see we was a-trabbelin' all night; didn't get here till daybreak; and Missy Florence and her ma is both sleepy."

"Oh, Hitty!" said Penny, "it's just like a dream."

"There, there," and the smiling black woman patted the little girl's shoulder. "I'm glad 'nuff to be here, and so's Missy Florence and her ma. Squire Dickinson and mistress they's gwine to stay up in Boston a spell longer."

"When Florence wakes up mayn't she come down and see me?" pleaded Penny.

"I reckon she will! I'll sure tell her what you say. Whatever you been a-doin' to your hair, Miss Penelope?" responded Hitty.

But Penny did not stop to answer; she was eager to tell her mother this wonderful news, and was running swiftly toward home.

Hitty stepped out on the porch and watched the little girl.

"Her hair do look somethin' dreadful," she said aloud, and then looked about with a smile of satisfaction. "Seems mighty good to be safe back again where we b'long," she declared, as she returned to her work.

Mrs. Balfour was as much surprised as even Penelope could wish at hearing of the return of part of the Dickinson family, and wondered, in her own thoughts, if this might not mean that the Americans were nearing a complete victory.

"And Florence is coming to see me. Can't I take Sylvia out to the wall and wait for her?" asked Penny.

"Yes, but tell Florence to come and see me before she goes home," responded Mrs. Balfour.

Penny established Sylvia as comfortably as an uneven stone wall would permit, and then sat watching for Florence. It was only two weeks since they had said good-bye, as they thought forever, on this very place; but as Penny thought of all that had happened since Florence gave her the chain and locket it seemed as if years had separated them.

Penny did not wait on the wall. The moment she saw Florence she started to run to meet her. Both the little girls were smiling, and Penny was the first to speak. "I'm so glad you are back, Florence."

"So am I," rejoined Florence. "But, oh, Penny——"

"Don't say a word about my hair. It's a secret," said Penny eagerly.

"But how can it be a secret? Everybody can see it!" responded the surprised Florence.

"I don't mean that. I mean the reason I cut it off is a secret," said Penelope. "Come to the wall and see Sylvia. Oh, Florence, I am so glad you are here. You don't suppose you will ever go away again, do you?"

"I don't believe we shall," replied Florence. "See, Penny!" and she held up Penny's golden coin, now fastened to a chain; "my father had it put on this chain, and I've worn it just as I promised."

"And I have worn your locket every minute. Let's keep the promise and always wear them, even if you didn't go to England," responded Penny, and Florence eagerly agreed.

There were so many things to tell each other that it was dinner-time before they had half finished; and Florence had to run home, promising to come again the following day.

"Mother, Florence says that she doesn't want her pony back," Penny announced as she and Ted came in all ready for the midday meal. "She told me to tell Ted that it was a truly present, and that her father was going to get her another one."

"Then I may keep it, mayn't I, mother?" said Ted.

"We won't decide on that just yet," responded Mrs. Balfour. "It was a very generous gift, and now that the Dickinsons are back perhaps you may not want to keep the pony, Ted."

Ted did not look up, or make any answer to this suggestion. He had become very fond of the white pony; and he almost wished the Dickinsons had gone to England if their return meant that he must give the little creature back.

"If the squire comes back he'll have to swear to be loyal to the American government," Ted said. "Any man who won't will have to leave Rhode Island."

"Well, we will wait and see what Squire Dickinson will do," Mrs. Balfour responded quietly; "but after you finish your dinner, Ted, you had best put on your Sunday clothes. Penny and I will put on our best gowns and we will all walk up to the Stone House and see Mrs. Dickinson and tell her how glad we are that she and Florence have returned safely."

Ted moved about uneasily, and muttered the word "Tories," but not in so low a tone but that his mother heard him.

"Theodore," she said sharply, "before you change your clothes harness the pony into the cart. I have decided that you cannot keep it."

"Oh, mother!" pleaded the boy.

But Mrs. Balfour did not relent. She was sure that Ted fully understood why she had so decided, and Ted was thoroughly ashamed of himself for the muttered word. But he felt it was a very hard punishment, and as he harnessed the pretty little creature the boy was as near tears as a boy of fourteen could be.

Both the children were very quiet on their way to Stone House. Ted would not ride, nor did he offer a seat to Penny or his mother. He led the pony, and Mrs. Balfour and Penelope walked along the foot-path by the side of the road.

Mrs. Dickinson gave them a warm welcome and repeated that the pony was Ted's property if he wished to keep it.

"You will let Theodore decide, won't you, Mrs. Balfour?" said Mrs. Dickinson, and Ted's mother answered quietly:

"Certainly, Mrs. Dickinson."

But Ted knew that by that whispered word against his neighbors he had forfeited the right to accept a favor from them, and said bravely:

"I'd like to keep the pony, Mrs. Dickinson, but I can't."

Mrs. Dickinson smiled and nodded. She thought she understood the reason, for she knew that the war had made the Balfours less prosperous than formerly, and she imagined that perhaps they could not afford to feed the little animal. So no more was said, and Ted and his mother soon started for home, but Penny was to stay for an hour or two with Florence.

Ted walked silently beside his mother until they reached their own gate; then as he held it open for her to pass through, he said quickly: "Mother, I'm awfully ashamed. It's all right not to keep the pony."

There were tears in Mrs. Balfour's eyes when she answered him.

"I knew you'd understand, Ted," she said.

CHAPTER XVII

THE SECRET IS TOLD

FLORENCE listened eagerly to Penny's account of her visit to Mrs. Godfrey. Penny did not have very much to say about Colonel Barton, for she was quite sure that Florence would not want to hear it; and whenever any reference was made to her short hair Penny immediately became silent.

"Now tell me everything that happened to you while you were away, Florence," said Penny one day nearly a week after Florence's return to Stone House. The two little girls were on the shore, near Ted's boat, and Penny had just explained that the boat's name had always been "Freedom."

"And nobody ever guessed it!" exclaimed Florence admiringly.

"Oh, yes; one man guessed it," said Penny, recalling the tall man from Tiverton.

"Who?" questioned Florence.

"I don't know. 'Twas a tall man I met one day," answered Penny. "You haven't told me a word, Florence, about what happened to you going to Boston," she concluded, a little reproachfully.

"Why, nothing happened!" responded Florence in a tone of surprise. "It was night, and I went to sleep, and then it was morning, and pretty soon we were in Boston."

"Was that all?" Penny's voice expressed so much disappointment that Florence almost wished that her grandfather's coach had been attacked by "rebels," or that some adventure worth recounting had befallen her.

"That's all," she acknowledged, "only that father was expecting us, and we stayed in a big brick house near the river."

"What did you do?" urged Penny. "Didn't you see any soldiers, or anything interesting?"

"Grandmother Dickinson taught me some embroidery stitches, and my father took me to walk on Boston Common," said Florence.

"Then I'd rather stay right here than go to Boston," declared Penny, "for more things than that happened here."

"Yes, you visited the minister's wife," agreed Florence.

"More than that," said Penny.

"You cut off your hair," said Florence.

"More than that," said Penny again, and at Florence's look of wondering surprise Penny could no longer resist the temptation to tell Florence her great secret: "I carried a message to Colonel Elliott. It was night, and I walked to the crossroads and back again. A tall man brought the letter, and told me to ask 'Sammy' to take it. I played I was 'Sammy.' I cut off my hair, and dressed in Ted's clothes. And nobody knows 'twas me."

For a moment neither of the little girls spoke. Then Florence said: "Then you helped capture General Prescott."

"I guess so," replied Penny; "anyway the message was for Colonel Elliott to come and get him. And after I got home and was fast asleep he did come, and carried General Prescott off in a coach; and I never saw him."

As Penny finished speaking there was a scrambling sound from the other side of the boat, a muttered exclamation, and Ted stumbled to his feet.

"Ted Balfour! You've been listening!" declared Penny angrily. "Yes, you have. You hid there on purpose, and now you have heard my secret. You ought to be ashamed." Penny looked very angry as she stood facing her brother.

Ted looked at her steadily. "I am ashamed," he answered, "ashamed of you, Pen Balfour! You stole my chance to take that message. You know you did. But I didn't hide there to listen," and the boy's face flushed angrily. "I was fast asleep, and when you began to talk it woke me and I thought I'd wait a minute and jump out and frighten you. And then I heard."

"I don't believe it. You listened," declared Penny.

Ted walked off toward the house without another word.

"He will tell mother. Florence, what shall I do?" exclaimed Penny, quite forgetting how proud she had been of her errand and its success.

The tide was coming up, and the water now lapped the stern of the "Freedom"; and as Penny looked at the boat a sudden resolve took possession of her.

"Get into the boat, Florence, quick!" she commanded, and Florence obeyed.

Penny now pushed the boat out into the water, sprang in after Florence, and began to row out of the little cove.

"Where are you going, Penny?" asked Florence.

"I'm going after my father," said Penny, "and I am going to find that tall man who brought back my sunbonnet."

"Will it take long to find them?" questioned Florence, a little fearfully.

"I don't know," said Penny.

At this Florence began to cry. She wished that she had not got into the boat. She suddenly remembered that Penny's father was a rebel soldier, and she wished with all her heart that she was with her mother at Stone House.

But Florence did not cry very long. The sun shone brightly, a pleasant air came over the smooth waters of the bay, and Penny looked very brave and unafraid. Perhaps Penny knew just where to find Mr. Balfour, thought Florence, and they would soon be home again.

As the boat shot out beyond the point and headed toward Prudence Island, Penny's anger began to cool, and she wished to herself that she had not accused Ted of listening.

"I don't believe Ted did listen," she announced suddenly.

"Of course he didn't," agreed Florence. "I guess he couldn't help hearing."

"I wish I hadn't said I didn't believe him," continued Penny, even more meekly.

"Well, you can tell him so when you go home," said Florence hopefully, "and, Penny, I ought to go home this minute. I'm afraid my mother won't want me to go so far in a boat."

Penny stopped rowing. "I didn't think about that. I'll take you right home," she said meekly, and in a short time the "Freedom" was fast at her accustomed landing, and the two little friends stood on the shore.

"Penny," began Florence, slipping her hand over her friend's, "I won't ever tell your secret, and, Penny, I don't believe Ted will either."

A little smile crept around Penny's mouth.

"Of course he won't," she responded. Penny was feeling very much ashamed of herself, but she hardly knew how to straighten out the tangle. "I don't want you to tell, not yet, Florence," she said, as she bade Florence good-bye and went toward home.

Ted did not look up or speak to Penny when she came into the house; but Penny was sure that he had not told their mother what he had overheard.

It seemed a very long day to the little girl. She did not find pleasure in playing with Sylvia. When she tried to knit on the woolen stocking she dropped stitches, forgot to count, and got her work in such a tangle that she had to take it to her mother to straighten out.

They were in their favorite seats under the big oak; Ted was busy in the garden. Penny watched her mother unravel her work.

"Mother," she exclaimed suddenly, "I'm just as miserable as I can be. I hate secrets."

Mrs. Balfour put the stocking down and drew Penelope into her lap. "Tell mother," she said gently, and Penny gladly told the whole story.

"And I hid the blue sunbonnet under a log," concluded the little girl, "and I guess Ted won't ever like me again."

"We must get the sunbonnet before it is completely spoiled," said Mrs. Balfour, "and as for Ted, why, my dear, 'a brother is born for adversity,'" she quoted, "and I think he will understand when I tell him all about it."

"Will you tell him, mother?" and Penny's voice sounded more hopeful.

"Yes, dear child. And we must agree not to have any more secrets," said Mrs. Balfour.

"Never any more!" agreed Penny earnestly. "I'll go and fetch Ted," she added, running off toward the garden.

It was a half hour later when Mrs. Balfour saw the brother and sister coming across the field together. They were talking earnestly, and Mrs. Balfour put down her work with a happy smile.

"I've told him," Penny called out as they came nearer.

"That's right, my dear," said Mrs. Balfour.

"Pen had good courage, didn't she, mother?" Ted said as the three talked over the troubled days that had passed. "I think she's earned the name of Sammy."

"I ought to have let Ted take the message," confessed Penny.

"It's all right; all in the family," rejoined Ted laughingly. "After supper we'd better go down and dig out that blue sunbonnet."

"I guess I'll stir up some spice cakes for supper," said their mother, rolling up her work and starting for the house, closely followed by the two children.

"Mother," exclaimed Ted suddenly, "there are two men out by our barn. See!"

"It's father!" exclaimed Penny. "It's father, and the tall man who brought back my sunbonnet," and it was Penny who was the first to reach her soldier father and be clasped in his arms. "Don't say a word about my hair. Don't, father!" pleaded the little girl, as she saw her father's disapproving look as it rested on her shorn head. But of course the story had to be retold. But this time Roger Sherwin, for that was the tall man's name, had so much to say in praise of Penelope's courage that the little girl began to feel quite proud of herself.

The supper table was spread with the best supper that Mrs. Balfour and Penny could prepare, and it was a happy party gathered around the board. Penny's father had a month's leave of absence, and Roger Sherwin was on his way to Connecticut. It was dark when he bade the Balfours good-bye and started on his journey.

"I shall see you again, little maid," he said to Penny. "You have been a good and faithful messenger in a good cause," and then he was gone.

"Say, Pen, we forgot all about the blue sunbonnet," said Ted. "We'll go down and get it to-morrow morning."

CHAPTER XVIII

A BIRTHDAY PARTY

"Glad to see your boat isn't ashamed of her name," said Mr. Balfour, when he and Ted went down to the shore and looked at the little boat.

"It wasn't being ashamed, it was just being careful, father," replied Ted, "and Pen and I used to think it was great fun to hear Squire Dickinson say that he thought 'Modeerf' was a fine name for a boat."

"I like it better the way it is now," said Mr. Balfour laughingly, "but I heard good news about young Mr. Dickinson, Florence's father. I was told that he had given up his position in the employ of the Crown and declared himself a loyal American."

"Perhaps the squire will change too," responded Ted hopefully. But Mr. Balfour shook his head doubtfully; he had little hope that the old squire would give up his lifelong convictions.

While Ted and his father made the boat ready for their fishing excursion Penny was very busy making a birthday present for Mrs. Godfrey, for that very morning Dilly had appeared at the Balfour farm with an invitation for Penny and Ted to come to the parsonage the next afternoon to Mrs. Godfrey's birthday party.

Dilly also had an invitation for Florence, who had come running over to say that she could go if Ted and Penny would go with her in the pony-cart. Mrs. Balfour had gladly given her consent, and, as soon as Dilly had set out on her return journey, Penny said:

"I do wish that I could make a birthday present for Mrs. Godfrey. Couldn't I, mother?"

"Of course you can," responded Mrs. Balfour, "but you will have to decide what you will make and begin at once, for you will not have much time."

"Couldn't I make her a sewing-bag?" Penny asked eagerly. "There are lots of pieces of the blue muslin."

"Yes, indeed," agreed her mother; "run up and get my piece-bag, and bring down the roll of cardboard from the lower drawer in the high-boy."

"I want to make it all myself," Penny said, as she spread out the cardboard and bits of muslin on the kitchen table, and Mrs. Balfour nodded her approval.

Penelope brought a small plate from the closet and laid it down on the cardboard; then taking her pencil she carefully marked around the plate's edge and then cut out the circle. Then she laid the pasteboard circle on the muslin and cut two muslin circles, each a little larger than the cardboard, and basted them carefully over the cardboard, turning in the edges, and felling them neatly together. This took some time; but before dinner was ready Penny had finished the bottom of the work-bag, and had cut out and basted the pockets on the strip of muslin that was to form the bag.

"I can finish it this afternoon," she said, when her mother told her that she must put away her sewing and call her father and Ted to dinner.

After the dinner dishes were washed, Penny took her work down to the seat under the oak tree, and it was not long before she saw Florence coming across the field. Florence carried a small work-bag, and when she saw that Penny was sewing busily she seemed greatly pleased.

"I'm making a present for Mrs. Godfrey," said Penny, as Florence sat down beside her.

"So am I!" responded Florence, drawing a small square of fine cambric from her work-bag. "See, I have hemstitched this handkerchief, and mother marked two 'G's' in this corner for me to embroider."

"It will be lovely!" declared Penny admiringly.

For a few moments the two little girls stitched busily without speaking, and then Florence said, "Penny, what do you think my father has done?"

"What?" responded Penny, looking up from her work in surprise, for Florence spoke in a very low tone as if she were not sure that she ought to speak at all.

"My father has changed his religion. He isn't a Tory any longer. He's an American," said Florence.

Penny looked at her little friend in amazement.

"That isn't religion," she said.

"What is it then?" demanded Florence.

Penny shook her head. "I don't exactly know," she confessed, "only 'tisn't religion. Religion is Presbyterian and Episcopal."

"Well, I thought 'twas religion," said Florence, "because grandpa said 'twas a very serious thing to do. But now 'tis done, and my father is coming here to live and be a citizen."

Penny looked at Florence in more surprise than ever.

"What's a 'citizen'?" she asked.

"It's what my father is going to be," replied Florence. "I don't really know what it is, but it is something splendid or my father wouldn't be it."

"Umm," responded Penelope a little doubtfully, thinking to herself that she would ask her father what a "citizen" really was. She wondered to herself if it might not be another word for "Tory."

Before supper-time the little work-bag and the pretty handkerchief were finished, and both the little girls were eager for the next day to come. Penny had told Florence about the wonderful white dogs, and the pretty black kittens, and Florence was looking forward to being introduced to "Pomp" and "Pride."

Early the next morning Ted was off to the woods, promising to be back before dinner-time. Penny wondered what Ted had gone after, and an hour before dinner started off to meet him. She was about half-way up the pasture slope when she heard his "Hulloa," and saw him coming. He was carrying something very careful-ly, and when Penny was near enough to see what it was she exclaimed admiringly:

"Oh, Ted, that is lovely! It's for Mrs. Godfrey, isn't it?"

"Of course it is," said Ted. "Do you think she will like it?"

"Better than anything!" declared Penny.

Ted was carrying an oval-shaped basket woven from small pliable branches of pine. It was filled with feath-ery green moss, and quantities of blossoming blue for-get-me-nots.

"I wanted to take her something," said Ted, and Penny again declared that his gift was beautiful.

Early in the afternoon the three children started for Mrs. Godfrey's. Ted's basket, carefully protected from the sun, was under the seat of the pony-cart, while Penny and Florence, with their gifts daintily wrapped, told Ted again that his gift would be the prettiest that Mrs. Godfrey could possibly have.

As Ted looked at the pretty white pony he gave a regretful sigh. But he had never said a word of his affec-tion for the little animal, nor of how sorry he was that he could no longer take care of it.

"This is where Mr. Roger Sherwin spoke to me," said Penny as they drove by the place where she had hid-den the sunbonnet.

"My mother says you are a little heroine," said Flo-rence, greatly to Penny's delight.

"That's what father says," declared Ted, and Penelope began to think that she was really the happiest girl in the world.

Mrs. Godfrey was expecting them, and there were a number of other children in the garden. There was Philip Perkins, who had brought the message from the minister on the day of Penny's visit, and several little girls and boys whom Penny had seen at Sunday-school.

Mrs. Godfrey seemed greatly pleased with the sewing-bag and handkerchief, but Ted's basket of moss and wild forget-me-nots she declared was the most beautiful gift that she had ever received.

Florence soon made friends with one of the little girls from the village, and Penelope found herself standing between two girls of about her own age whose names she did not know. One of them looked at her so sharply that Penny became rather uncomfortable.

"You're the girl who said that verse about the islands right out loud in Sunday-school," said one, looking at Penny with an unpleasant little smile.

"There was no harm in the verse; but I——" began Penny, but before she could finish the other girl said sharply:

"Yes, and you are the girl who cut off your hair and dressed up in boys' clothes. Come, Nancy, I guess we don't want to play with her," and with a scornful look over her shoulder the tall girl and her companion moved away.

Penelope looked after them in angry surprise. She had forgotten all about the verse, and she was quite sure that in carrying the message she had done a service to be proud of. But to be scorned by two girls seemed very hard. Just then she heard a pleasant voice speak her name, and she turned to find Mrs. Arnold smiling at her.

"I think you and I ought to be friends, Miss Penelope Balfour," said Mrs. Arnold, "for you and I sent that message to Colonel Elliott. You were a brave girl to come to my house that night. Now come with me to the sitting-room where Mrs. Godfrey has a fine new game for us to play," and taking Penny by the hand she led her toward the house, apparently not noticing Penny's unhappy silence.

In a few moments all the children were in the sitting-room. "There is just time for a game before supper," Mrs. Godfrey announced. "Draw your chairs close together in a circle. Now, no one must speak or laugh. The one who breaks this rule will have to stand in the corner, face to the wall, for five minutes."

The children smiled at each other. But when Penny found her chair next to the tall girl who had spoken so rudely to her in the garden she was almost tempted to speak so that she could go and stand with her face to the wall, for she was sure that would be more pleasant than sitting next to Ann Maria Talbot.

"Penelope Balfour, you are to be the leader in the game," announced Mrs. Godfrey, with her charming smile, and Penny smiled back, and began to feel her happy self once more. What did she care for Ann Marias or Nancys as long as Mrs. Godfrey was her friend? "Penelope," went on Mrs. Godfrey, "you are to tap your neighbor's knee, your neighbor on the right. She is to tap her neighbor, and so on around the circle back to the leader. Then Penny will begin and tap both of Ann Maria's knees. The third time round she will tap both knees and one cheek; the fourth time both knees and both cheeks. The fifth time Penny will take hold of her neighbor's ear and all the circle will do the same. And," concluded Mrs. Godfrey, "if no one has laughed or said a word by that time I shall think that you are all very remarkable children."

Penny was sure now that she would enjoy the game, and looked forward to the moment when she could tweak Ann Maria's ear. Florence was on Penny's other side. The game began by Penny's giving Ann Maria's knee a sharp tap. The whole circle was smiling and interested, and when it was time to tap Ann Maria's cheek Penny's tap was almost a slap. Ann Maria winced and gave her neighbor an angry glance. When the time came for the tweak of the ear, however, Ann Maria's patience was exhausted and she jumped up exclaiming, "I don't like this game. I didn't come here to be slapped by Penny Balfour."

The other children looked at her in horrified surprise. To be rude at a party, at the minister's wife's party at that, seemed an almost unbelievable thing. But Mrs. Godfrey did not seem to mind.

"So Ann Maria has lost the game," she said pleasantly, "and she will have to stand facing the wall for five minutes. As you are all polite and well-brought-up children, I know you will not want Ann Maria to stand alone, so let us all stand face to the wall with her," and Mrs. Godfrey faced about toward the wall. The children laughingly obeyed.

"Isn't Mrs. Godfrey an angel?" Florence whispered to Penny as they walked together out to the dining-room where Dilly stood smiling at each little guest, and all ready to help them to the delicious little biscuit, preserved fruit, creamed potatoes and chicken.

In the center of the table was the big round birthday cake with its pink candles. When the children had finished with the other dainties Mrs. Godfrey lighted the candles.

"Florence," said Mrs. Godfrey, "you are to blow out the first candle, and make a wish aloud; then the rest of you are to follow in the same way."

Florence obeyed a little timidly, blowing out the candle and then making a little bow to Mrs. Godfrey she said, "I wish you many happy birthdays."

There was a little murmur of approval from all the other guests, and as each one blew out a candle they, too, bowed and said, "I wish you happiness."

CHAPTER XIX

A YOUNG BEAR

"WE must plan for a day in the blueberry pasture. The berries are at their best now, and I want to dry as many as possible this year," said Mrs. Balfour the day after Mrs. Godfrey's birthday party. "I think we had better go to-morrow," she concluded.

The blueberry pasture was about a mile distant from the Balfour farm, and every summer the family made a day's excursion to gather the berries. They carried a picnic dinner, and Penny and Ted always thought it one of the most pleasant excursions of the summer.

The berries were made into pies, blueberry sauce, and preserves; and beside these Mrs. Balfour always spread a large quantity of berries to dry on papers on the attic floor. These dried berries were very appetizing in the long winter months, and were used in puddings, cakes and cookies.

"Mother, may I ask Florence to go with us?" said Penny.

"Yes, and perhaps Mrs. Dickinson may like to go. You may run up and ask them," responded Mrs. Balfour. "Tell them that we want to make an early start, and that we plan to stay all day."

Penny ran off toward Stone House. Mr. and Mrs. Balfour watched her with smiling faces.

"Penny feels as if she had helped win a great triumph for the American cause," said Mrs. Balfour. "Ever since she confessed her part in carrying the message she has been as happy as a lark."

"She really did Colonel Barton a great service," said Mr. Balfour. "Sherwin says that by Penny's not speaking of the message, and obeying his directions exactly there was not much danger of discovery. I am proud of the child's courage."

"They are both good children, and if the war were over we could indeed be happy," responded Mrs. Balfour.

" 'Tis practically over now," declared Mr. Balfour. "I dare say by another summer Colonel Sullivan will have ten thousand loyal men in Rhode Island, and a French fleet in Narragansett Bay to drive out the British ships; and then we shall have little to trouble us."

Mrs. Dickinson said that she and Florence would enjoy the excursion to the blueberry pasture and would be on hand early the next morning.

"My father will be here very soon," said Florence, "and I know what a 'citizen' is. A citizen is a man who obeys the laws he helps to make," and Florence looked very proud of having discovered such an important piece of knowledge.

"That is what a good citizen does," added Mrs. Dickinson, "such a citizen as Penny's father."

Penny gave a little sigh of relief. If Mr. Dickinson was coming back to Stone House because he intended to be like her father, Penny was sure that all would be well.

The next morning was clear and pleasant, and Ted and his mother had just finished packing the basket of luncheon when Mrs. Dickinson and Florence appeared.

Mrs. Dickinson carried a covered basket, evidently well filled, while Florence had two baskets woven of grass and rushes. These baskets were made by the Indians, many of whom still wandered about the shores of Narragansett Bay, and who now and then visited the houses of the settlers to exchange their baskets for food or clothing.

Florence wore a neat gingham dress and sunbonnet. Since her return from Boston she no longer was dressed in embroidered white dresses and dainty shoes.

"You'll have better times now, Florence," Penny said approvingly, "because you won't have to be so careful of your dress."

The little party made their way along the pleasant path through the pine woods, crossed an open field and then reached the pasture where the blueberries grew in great abundance.

"We had better decide where we will have luncheon and put the lunch baskets there before we begin to pick berries," said Mr. Balfour.

"Amethyst Brook is the best place," declared Ted, leading the way up a little slope covered with young

pine trees, to where a big chestnut tree made a pleasant shade, and where Amethyst Brook came dashing
over its rocky bed in a foamy waterfall.

"I did not know there was such a beautiful place as
this so near Stone House," said Mrs. Dickinson, as Ted
took her lunch basket and put it among the cool ferns
near the brook.

The blueberry bushes grew all up the slope, and were
covered with ripe berries, and in a few minutes they
were all picking, calling now and then to each other.

Penelope and Florence kept close together, and followed the brook where it came down across the pasture.
They talked over the birthday party, and Penny con-
fided to Florence that she really had "slapped," instead
of tapped, the cheek of Ann Maria Talbot.

"And I'm not a mite sorry, not a single mite," said
Penny, "for she wasn't polite."

"Served her right," agreed Florence, "but I don't
believe she had a very good time."

"Horrid people never do have good times," said
Penny firmly. "I know that, because when I do hateful things I spoil all my good times."

They soon filled their baskets and carried them to the
big chestnut tree and emptied them into the large baskets, and then started out again.

"Don't go far away, children," called Mr. Balfour.

"There are splendid berries on the other side of the
brook," said Penny, as the two little girls made their
way along the bank of the stream.

"But we couldn't get across," responded Florence. "There are all those sharp rocks, and it's deep."

"We could take off our shoes and stockings and wade. Come on, Florence, let's do it. The water would be so cool and nice."

Florence was usually quite ready to do anything that Penny might suggest, but she looked at the rushing water a little doubtfully. But Penny's shoes and stockings were off, and Florence followed her example.

"We'll carry them in our baskets," said Penny, wading boldly in. Florence followed, and the stream was crossed without any adventure. The girls dried their feet on the warm moss, put on their shoes and stockings, and began filling their baskets again.

The bushes grew very thick, and as they pushed their way further in they soon were out of the sound of the brook; but they were talking busily, exclaiming over the size and ripeness of the berries, and not until their baskets were filled did they think of their whereabouts.

"There are blueberry bushes everywhere," said Florence suddenly. "I can't see any brook."

"But I can see the big tree," said Penny, "and we might as well start back. It must be 'most time for luncheon."

"The tree seems further and further away, doesn't it, Penny?" said Florence in a tired voice, after they had been pushing their way among the bushes for a long time.

"I can't see it at all!" exclaimed Penny. They now came out from the bushes to an open stretch of rocky ground. Just beyond this was a thick growth of pine trees. "I don't know this place at all," said Penny. "I guess we'd better go back the way we came."

"I don't want to go back into those bushes," said Florence. "If we climb up on that ledge perhaps we can see where the brook is."

"Perhaps we can," agreed Penny hopefully, and the two little girls clambered up over the rocks until they reached the summit of the ledge.

"It's just woods everywhere, isn't it, Penny?" said Florence. "What isn't blueberry bushes is woods. I'm dreadful thirsty."

The July sun beat down hotly on the rocks, and after looking vainly for some familiar landmark the girls left the ledge and sat down to rest in the shadow of a high rock. They ate blueberries from their baskets, and talked about the luncheon in the baskets under the big chestnut tree.

"Hitty made some sugar cookies," said Florence, "and there were cup custards too."

"And mother made ginger bread," added Penny, "and Ted was going to build a fire to roast potatoes."

Then there was a little silence. The girls both looked at their baskets of berries, but they no longer tasted them. Penny was thinking to herself that she should never again like the taste of blueberries.

"Penny, are we lost?" Florence's voice sounded very near to tears, and Penny suddenly remembered that

A Round Furry Head Appeared

Florence had not wanted to cross the brook; and said to herself that if they were lost and starved to death it would be all her fault.

"I guess we are, Florence," she answered, "but we needn't be afraid, for father and Ted won't let us stay lost."

Florence leaned her head against Penny's shoulder. "I'm awful tired," she said, and in a moment her eyes closed and she was fast asleep.

Penny sat very still. Although she had spoken bravely to Florence about her father and Ted finding them she was by no means certain that this would be the case.

"They won't think of our crossing the brook. I don't see what made me," she said to herself. "Anyway, I must take care of Florence," she resolved.

A little scrambling noise among the rocks in front of where the little girls sat attracted Penny's attention, and she looked quickly in the direction of the sound. "Oh!" she exclaimed and then sat very still, hardly daring to breathe, for a round furry head appeared above the rocks, then two black paws, and finally an animal which looked to Penny like a big brown dog came jumping toward them. The berry baskets were directly in front of the girls, and when the animal reached the baskets he plunged his nose in and began to eat the berries eagerly.

"Dogs don't eat blueberries," Penny thought to herself, and suddenly remembered hearing her father say that very morning that the bears and their cubs would have a feast of blueberries this year. "It's a cub! It's a young bear!" she thought to herself. But she did not move.

The cub devoured the contents of Penny's basket, and then with an appreciative grunt stuck his nose into the other. Florence's basket had a handle across the middle of the basket and another running lengthwise. So it was rather difficult for the cub to get at the berries. He persevered, however, until his head was well under the handles; and now his troubles began, for he could not get his head free. He began to claw at it with his paws, and to thrash about making angry noises.

"Oh, Penny, what is it?" exclaimed Florence, jumping up wide awake.

"It's a bear cub; we must run," answered Penny, grasping Florence by the hand and pulling her along over the rough ground. The young bear was too much occupied with his own troubles to care what the strange looking creatures did; and Penny and Florence had crossed the open space and plunged into the thicket on the other side long before young Bruin was free again.

The girls ran on, breathless and frightened until a familiar sound made Penny stop.

"Listen! That's the brook, Florence!" she exclaimed, "and I was sure we were running right away from it."

"Don't stop to take off shoes," panted Florence, as they came to the bank a little distance above the waterfall. Penny waded in and Florence after her; and then tired and hungry they made their way to the chestnut tree.

Ted was just preparing a fire near the brook, while Mrs. Balfour and Mrs. Dickinson were taking the food from the baskets.

"Your father has just gone to look for you," said Mrs. Balfour, and then noticing their tired faces and soaked shoes she exclaimed: "For pity's sake, children, where have you been?"

Before Penny had finished the story Mr. Balfour appeared, and Penny knew by the expression on his face that they had been in great danger. "It was all my fault," she said; "if the bear had eaten us it would have been my fault. Florence did not want to cross the brook and I made her."

"Is it only noon?" asked Florence in a surprised voice. "I thought that we had been away hours and hours, and that it must be almost night."

"And the bear got our baskets," said Penny regretfully.

"The bear is quite welcome to the baskets," declared Mr. Balfour, clasping Penny's hand close in his own and keeping very near to her the remainder of the day.

It was a very quiet party that made their way back to Balfour farm in the late afternoon. Mrs. Dickinson kissed Penny when she said good-night, greatly to the little girl's surprise. The big baskets were well filled with berries. Ted declared they had never brought home as many before.

"And we would have had more if it hadn't been for that young bear," said Penny regretfully.

CHAPTER XX

PENNY AND CAPTAIN BALFOUR

"Everything seems to happen to Pen," said Ted, as he and his father were at work in the garden the morning after the blueberry excursion. "It was Pen who found that letter of the squire's, it was Pen who carried Colonel Barton's message, and now it's Pen who has seen a bear cub. She pulled me out of the water, too, this summer. If Pen hadn't have known just what to do I guess I would have drowned," he concluded.

This was the first that Mr. Balfour had heard of Ted's rescue, and he listened to the story saying, as Ted described Penny's promptness and presence of mind, that there were greater dangers than bears after all.

"I was thinking," explained Ted, with a laugh, "that all Pen's adventures ought to have been mine. I ought to have saved her life, and I ought to have found the letter, and carried the message, and met the bear."

"I hope Penelope's adventures are over," said Mr. Balfour, "and that from now on she will walk in safety and peace."

"Oh, Pen likes to have things happen," declared Ted, "and so do I."

"I wish I were sure of being at home after this," said Mr. Balfour. "I begin to think that my family needs me more than my regiment."

"Father," interrupted Ted eagerly, "who is that man on horseback stopping at our gate?"

Mr. Balfour did not recognize the visitor at first, but as he went toward the road, closely followed by Ted, he exclaimed:

"It's Dickinson, young Dickinson!"

The two neighbors greeted each other cordially. "I have a letter for you, Mr. Balfour," said Mr. Dickinson, drawing a packet from his breast pocket, "and I hope it brings good news," and after a few more words he rode on toward Stone House.

Ted watched his father as he broke the seal and read the letter, and when he saw the smile on his father's face Ted smiled too.

"Our neighbor has indeed brought good news. This letter is from Roger Sherwin. He says that the American cause is winning friends everywhere, and what else do you think he says?" and Mr. Balfour smiled at Ted's eager face.

"What? What, father?"

"He says that your father, Peter Charles Balfour, is to receive a commission as captain in the regiment stationed at Warwick Neck."

Ted could hardly speak for delight. "Captain Peter Balfour," he almost whispered; then repeated it in a louder tone, and at last fairly shouted it as he ran toward the house to tell his mother and Penny the good news.

"That means that I can be near home, probably, until peace is declared," said "Captain" Balfour, "and I think Penelope deserves to have an American officer in her family."

"We ought to celebrate this day," said Mrs. Balfour proudly.

"I suppose Mrs. Dickinson would agree with that, since it is the day of her husband's return," replied Captain Balfour laughingly.

"May I go and tell Florence?" asked Penny, who, with Sylvia in her arms, had listened eagerly to this wonderful news.

Mrs. Balfour gave her consent, and Penny started off toward Stone House. She was halfway across the field when a strange sound from the road made her stop suddenly and look in that direction.

"Oh!" exclaimed Penny.

Down the road toward Balfour farm came a little procession. At the head was a drummer, and the smooth even music of the drum made Penny's feet move in time; and when the notes of a fife joined the little girl exclaimed again.

Behind the men playing the drum and fife marched another man carrying the American flag, and then came a number of men from Warwick Village.

"They are coming to our house," exclaimed Penny, as the musicians struck up a livelier tune, and stopped at the front gate leading to the Balfour house.

As Penny stood watching this wonderful appearance, she heard her name spoken, and there was Florence close beside her.

"It's because my father is a brave soldier," Penny whispered, clasping Florence's hand, and feeling ready to cry.

"There are your father and mother at the front door," said Florence, "and there's Ted." And the two little girls watched the Warwick men enter the gate, and shake Captain Balfour by the hand.

"There comes a carriage; two carriages!" said Penny. "One is the minister's carriage," and they saw the carriages drive into the farmyard, and several women dismount, taking out boxes and packages. "Come on, Florence," said Penny, and they ran swiftly toward the farmhouse just in time to hear Mrs. Godfrey say to Penny's mother:

"Mrs. Arnold and Mrs. Green and I thought you would not be ready for so many visitors, so we brought a pie or two; and Dilly came to help."

"A pie or two," responded Mrs. Balfour laughingly, as she saw Dilly taking out a boiled ham, a number of roasted chickens, and a basket filled with biscuit.

Then what a busy time there was! Tablecloths were spread on the smooth grass under the big tree, and while Dilly and Ted brought the food from the carriages Mrs. Balfour and her friends carved the ham and chickens, and brought pitchers of cool milk from the dairy.

In the midst of the preparations Penny saw her father and the minister start for Stone House.

"They have gone to get your father, Florence," said Ted, coming up to where the girls were standing; and when Mr. and Mrs. Dickinson were seen returning with Captain Balfour and Mr. Godfrey there was a little murmur of applause and the drum and fife sounded a gay welcome.

"Isn't it splendid, Penny?" whispered Florence. The two little girls had kept a little distance from the older people, feeling as if it was all a wonderful game arranged for their pleasure. Before Penelope could answer she felt a gentle touch on her shoulder, and looked up to see Mrs. Arnold smiling down at her.

"I thought this was my little messenger," said the kind woman; "now you two little girls must come and sit with me, where we can get a bite to eat and hear all the nice things these Warwick men have to say about your fathers," and she led them to where Mrs. Godfrey was sitting; and now for the first time Penny saw that there were a number of children sitting quietly near the big tree.

"Here are some of your friends from the village, Penelope," said Mrs. Godfrey. "Here are Nancy and Ann Maria Talbot."

The Talbot girls did not look as if they were very happy. But Penny was so happy herself that she forgot all about their former unkindness and welcomed them warmly.

"Our father plays the drum," said Ann Maria, in so meek a voice that Penny looked at her in surprise.

Then, after the luncheon was finished, Mr. Godfrey stood up and said many true and pleasant things about the honor and courage of American soldiers, and of the especial valor of Colonel William Barton and his daring capture of General Prescott. Penny listened eagerly. Suddenly she realized that the minister was telling the story of Penelope Balfour carrying a message through the darkness to Warwick Village and then she heard him say that she was the brave daughter of a brave soldier. Then there was a clapping of hands, and the drum and fife began to play, and Penny felt as if she were going to cry, and was very glad that Ann Maria Talbot had heard what the minister said.

But the proudest and happiest moment for Penny and for Florence came when Captain Balfour thanked Mr. Godfrey and his Warwick friends, and said that the real occasion for this friendly gathering was to welcome home a good neighbor and a loyal citizen, Edward Dickinson.

It was late in the afternoon when the drum and fife sounded the call to march, and the Warwick neighbors went gayly down the road toward their homes. The flag waved over them, the music rose and fell, and at the gate of the Balfour farm Penny, Florence and Ted stood watching and listening until the flag was out of sight and the music had died away. Then as they turned back toward the house Ted stopped suddenly and pointed toward the field. Black Aleck, leading the white pony harnessed to the pony-cart, was coming toward the Balfour farm.

"There comes your pony, Florence," said Ted.

Florence shook her head. "It's your pony, Ted; father says so," she answered. "You will have to keep it this time."

Ted looked toward his mother questioningly, and as she smiled and nodded, Ted smiled in response as he said:

"I'm glad enough to keep him, Florence, and I can't thank you enough."

Penny walked with Florence as far as the wall.

"Hasn't it been a wonderful day, Penny?" Florence said, as she slid down on the further side of the wall and looked back at her friend, "and I'm so glad I'm going to live neighbor to you."

"Yes, I'm glad too, Florence," responded Penny, touching her little gold locket tenderly, "and I'm glad we're both Americans."